Erratum
Evil Online
Dean Cocking and Jeroen van den Hoven
ISBN: 9781405154376 (pbk)
ISBN: 9781405154369 (hbk)

The publisher notes the following error in the print edition of *Evil Online* by Dean Cocking and Jeroen van den Hoven.

The sentence in chapter 1, page 15, paragraph 2, lines 7–9, was incorrectly printed as follows:

> In a toxic mixture of alcohol, drugs, social media, smartphones, and fraternity "partying," the most horrible things happened, yet were given a relatively light touch by soshed."[21]

This sentence should read:

> In a toxic mixture of alcohol, drugs, social media, smartphones, and fraternity "partying," the most horrible things happened, yet were given a relatively light touch by social media.[21]

This has now been corrected in the electronic versions of the book available online, and will be corrected in future reprints. The publisher apologizes for this error and any confusion that it may have caused.

Evil Online

Blackwell Public Philosophy
Edited by Michael Boylan, Marymount University

In a world of 24-hour news cycles and increasingly specialized knowledge, the Blackwell Public Philosophy series takes seriously the idea that there is a need and demand for engaging and thoughtful discussion of topics of broad public importance. Philosophy itself is historically grounded in the public square, bringing people together to try to understand the various issues that shape their lives and give them meaning. This "love of wisdom" – the essence of philosophy – lies at the heart of the series. Written in an accessible, jargon-free manner by internationally renowned authors, each book is an invitation to the world beyond newsflashes and soundbites and into public wisdom.

1. *Permission to Steal: Revealing the Roots of Corporate Scandal*
   by Lisa H. Newton
2. *Doubting Darwin? Creationist Designs on Evolution*
   by Sahotra Sarkar
3. *The Extinction of Desire: A Tale of Enlightenment*
   by Michael Boylan
4. *Torture and the Ticking Bomb*
   by Bob Brecher
5. *In Defense of Dolphins: The New Moral Frontier*
   by Thomas I. White
6. *Terrorism and Counter-Terrorism: Ethics and Liberal Democracy*
   by Seumas Miller
7. *Who Owns You? The Corporate Gold Rush to Patent Your Genes*
   by David Koepsell
8. *Animalkind: What We Owe to Animals*
   by Jean Kazez
9. *In the Name of God: The Evolutionary Origins of Religious Ethics and Violence*
   by John Teehan
10. *The Secular Outlook: In Defense of Moral and Political Secularism*
    by Paul Cliteur
11. *Freedom of Religion and the Secular State*
    by Russell Blackford
12. *As Free and as Just as Possible: The Theory of Marxian Liberalism*
    by Jeffrey Reiman
13. *Happy-People-Pills For All*
    by Mark Walker
14. *Life, Liberty, and the Pursuit of Dao*
    by Sam Crane
15. *The Justification of Religious Violence*
    by Steve Clarke
16. *Who Owns You? Science, Innovation, and the Gene Patent Wars*
    by David Koepsell

For further information about individual titles in the series, supplement ary material, and regular updates, visit www.blackwellpublishing.com/publicphilosophy

Evil Online

Dean Cocking
Jeroen van den Hoven

WILEY Blackwell

This edition first published 2018

Registered Offices
John Wiley & Sons, Inc., 111 River Street, Hoboken, NJ 07030, USA
John Wiley & Sons Ltd, The Atrium, Southern Gate, Chichester, West Sussex, PO19 8SQ, UK

Editorial Office
9600 Garsington Road, Oxford, OX4 2DQ, UK

For details of our global editorial offices, customer services, and more information about Wiley products visit us at www.wiley.com.

Wiley also publishes its books in a variety of electronic formats and by print-on-demand. Some content that appears in standard print versions of this book may not be available in other formats.

Library of Congress Cataloging-in-Publication Data

Name: Cocking, Dean, 1958– author.
Title: Evil online / by Dean Cocking, Jeroen van den Hoven.
Description: Hoboken : Wiley, 2018. | Series: Blackwell public philosophy |
Includes bibliographical references and index. |
Identifiers: LCCN 2017060972 (print) | LCCN 2018006550 (ebook) |
ISBN 9781119471202 (pdf) | ISBN 9781119471189 (epub) |
ISBN 9781405154369 (cloth) | ISBN 9781405154376 (pbk.)
Subjects: LCSH: Good and evil–Electronic information resources. |
Internet–Moral and ethical aspects.
Classification: LCC BJ1401 (ebook) | LCC BJ1401 .C57 2018 (print) | DDC 170–dc23
LC record available at https://lccn.loc.gov/2017060972

Cover Image: © DimaChe/Gettyimages
Cover Design: Wiley

Set in size of 10.5/13.5pt MinionPro by SPi Global, Pondicherry, India

Printed in Great Britain by TJ International Ltd, Padstow, Cornwall

10 9 8 7 6 5 4 3 2 1

In memory of my mother "Bonnie"
Dean Cocking

Ter nagedachtenis aan mijn vader
Jeroen van den Hoven

Contents

Acknowledgments

This book has been in progress for a number of years and much has happened along the way. Hence, we apologize in advance to those who have helped us, but whom we have forgotten to thank. Three research assistants have helped us over the course of writing the manuscript: Job Timmermans provided some excellent work on cyberbullying, and on online social worlds, in the early days of the project; Sofia Kaliarnta also gave us some excellent work on online trends and cases for Chapter 1 and David van Putten provided us with many helpful corrections and suggestions throughout. The book has also benefited from careful readings given by Justin Oakley and Robert Young. We are grateful for their many suggestions that helped develop our thoughts, and the many revisions that helped us avoid some embarrassing mistakes.

We are indebted to the Department of of Values, Technology and Innovation: Delft University of Technology, for their support of the project. In addition to supporting the work of our research assistants, Dean was also provided with a six-month fellowship to work on the project. We would also like to thank our editor at Wiley-Blackwell, Michael Boylan, for his strong support and encouragement in the early days, and his significant help over the past year. We are also very grateful to Alec McAulay for his excellent, collaborative and extensive copy-editing work and to Sindhuja Kumar whose proof-reading and production editing also improved the book significantly.

For their love and support Dean would like to thank his wife, Kylie Cocking, and their children, Harry, Chloe, Georgia, and Lola. Kylie and Dean have also spent much of their time over the past decade or so discussing this project. As a result, Kylie has initiated and helped develop many lines of thought in this book. Chapters 3, 4 and 5 are especially indebted to her contributions. Jeroen would also like to thank his family for their support: his wife Eugenie and his son Allard and daughter Emilie. To Emilie we are also grateful for providing us with some striking cases and examples. Jeroen would also like to thank his colleagues in Delft who have heard a lot about a project on evil and the Internet for a number of years, and not given up hope that it would appear.

Emblematic Still Life with Flagon, Glass, Jug and Bridle,
Johannes Torrentius, 1614

Preface

In the Rijksmuseum in Amsterdam hangs the seventeenth-century still life painting you can see on your left. It is by a painter named Torrentius, a contemporary of Vermeer, who, according to some who had been in a position to compare their work, was the better and technically more skilled painter of the two. Torrentius's ability to paint still life realistically was allegedly so impressive that some thought he had come to an agreement with the devil. The choice of topics of his paintings was also extraordinary: He was accused of and convicted for painting downright pornographic images.

What we know about Torrentius we mainly know through the proceedings of the many court cases that were brought against him because of his pornography. In Holland he had a group of enthusiastic followers and friends sometimes referred to as "Torrentians." They had outspoken ideas about good and evil, and one of their central lines of thought was that they were beyond good and evil. Torrentius himself is reported to have behaved and justified his actions as if he was the sole measure of good and evil.

The still life in Amsterdam is the only remaining painting by Torrentius. The painting is in the genre of the temperance movement, a symbolic reminder of the virtues of temperance and restraint. It depicts a horse bridle, two vases, a glass and a music score and the following text in Dutch: "*wat buyten maets bestaet in onmaets quaat vergaet*," which translates as "what fails to keep measure, will perish by extreme evil." Torrentius lived his life in stark contrast to this pictorial evocation of temperance. He was well known in his hometown Haarlem for his luxurious life style, parties and expensive extravagancies. To this end, the painting should probably be interpreted as an ironic statement.

Among the many who were friends or followers of Torrentius was Jeronimus Cornelisz, a disgruntled drugstore owner in Haarlem. Cornelisz had nothing to lose in Holland and embarked upon the *Batavia*, a ship of the *Vereenigde Oost-Indische Compagnie* (the Dutch East India Company), to set sail to Batavia, the capital of the Dutch territories in the Indonesian Archipelago. The ship carried a valuable cargo of jewelry, silver and gold coins. Some of the men on board had been planning a mutiny from the moment the ship left port in Amsterdam, intending to disappear with the cargo and start a new life somewhere in the Asian Pacific Region. Jeronimus Cornelisz was one of them.

They would have carried out their plans if the *Batavia* had not been thrown on to a reef in a storm near the western coast of Australia at the Houtman Abrolhos Islands. The sailors, officers and other people on board were able to reach a group of small coral islands. Here they stayed for a few months, while others in a small rowing boat went to get help. Cornelisz became the leader of the small stranded community of 150 people, many of whom were women and children desperately needing assistance. Instead, however, Cornelisz and his men imposed a reign of terror and went on a killing spree. In a couple of months more than 120 people were murdered, including women and children. According to eye witnesses who survived and were later rescued, the killings often seemed to be done just for the fun of it.

The shocking story of the Batavia has been evocatively described in several novels and books, and presents an explosive mixture of contextual features that are conducive to the flourishing of evil. First, there was an underlying self-serving motive of stealing and running with the riches that the ship carried. Second, there was the Torrentian philosophy of being above the law, beyond good and evil, and being entitled to set moral standards irrespective of what history had handed down and what existing social and legal institutions imposed. Third, there was the physical isolation of a coral reef island in one of the most remote corners of the world, untouched by man, but also unregulated, unobserved and so seemingly immune from censure.

In many cases, evil online has flourished in similar ways. Attitudes and conduct are set in new worlds where the nature and application of legal and moral values and constraints are far less clear and certain. There are new environments where the voice of moral authorities and the constraints of existing social institutions are often too weak to be heard, and where isolation from the reactions of others is ubiquitous. As a result, and unsurprisingly, those already guided by antisocial and immoral attitudes have been able to run amok online. The flourishing of evil online, however, is far from confined to the "likely suspects." It is not just the bad, mad or criminal that we have to worry about. On the contrary, much evil online is being driven, and engaged in, by otherwise relatively normal, ordinary people. People who have not already largely abandoned prosocial standards and moral values, and who otherwise have managed to conduct themselves in relatively prosocial ways. Trying to better understand this territory of evildoing, both online and in our traditional worlds, is the main focus of our book.

Thinking of evildoers as not radically dissimilar in psychology to most of us is nothing new; it has a long history and has been expressed in different and conflicting ways. So, for example, some philosophers, such as the Confucian, Xunzi, have claimed that we are all naturally evil,[1] whereas the Western philosopher, Immanuel Kant, thought that while we have the potential to exercise self-governance by morality, our self-conceit and our tendency to pursue self-interest at the expense of others is all too common.[2] Typically, tragedy also paints a

---

[1] For a thoughtful and accessible account of Xunzi's philosophy, see David Elstein's entry, Xunzi, *Internet Encyclopedia of Philosophy*, www.iep.utm.edu/xunzi (accessed 18 November 2017).

[2] Kant regarded an evil will simply and broadly in terms of failing to have a good will. See, Immanuel Kant, Religion within the boundaries of mere reason, in *Religion and Rational Theology* (translators and editors Allen W. Wood and George Di Giovanni), Cambridge: Cambridge University Press, 1996. Kant does describe different kinds of evil wills as more and less evil. The worst kind of will is where one is *governed* by self-interest, and so generally indifferent to conflict with the moral law. As we say above, for Kant our propensity to put ourselves ahead of others (our self-conceit) is all too

somber picture of the world and what we can know about it, a place where evildoing becomes unavoidable, or at least a common pitfall of our normal lives.[3] And, more recently, as we discuss in our final chapters, an industry in social science has emerged, investigating the evildoing of ordinary, even otherwise seemingly well-adjusted, people.

The most influential contemporary description of evildoing resulting from minds that are not already consumed by antisocial and immoral attitudes, has been Hannah Arendt's account of the "banality of evil." On this account, or a common reading of it, otherwise relatively normal people, not already driven, say, by malice or hatred for others, become evildoers because they are fundamentally unthinking and uncritical about their own conduct. In the face of seemingly loud and clear evidence to the contrary, banal evildoers manage to persist in being guided by very ordinary, widely shared attitudes and pursuits. Attitudes and pursuits that have morally neutral descriptions, such as "doing one's job well." They possess, Arendt said, "an inability to think, namely to think from the standpoint of someone else."[4]

Much of the rise of evil online may be seen as providing spectacularly new and widespread ways in which evil is banal and can flourish. However, there is typically much more to say about, and deeper considerations to explain, being "unthinking" about the moral status of one's conduct and how this can enable evildoing. What is true, we argue, is that evildoing is typically not motivated by the recognition that what one is doing is evil. Evildoers rarely aim at evil. The sadist

common, and in this sense he described our evildoing as radical. See also, for example, Claudia Card, Kant's theory of radical evil, in Claudia Card, *The Atrocity Paradigm: A Theory of Evil*, New York: Oxford University Press, 2002, pp. 73–95; Erik M. Hanson's entry, Immanuel Kant: Radical evil, Internet Encyclopedia of Philosophy, http://www.iep.utm.edu/rad-evil (accessed 18 November 2017); and Paul Formosa, Kant on the radical evil of human nature, *The Philosophical Forum*, 38, no. 3, 2007, pp. 221–246.

[3] For an account of evil in terms of tragedy see, John Kekes, *Facing Evil*, Princeton, NJ, Princeton University Press, 1990.

[4] Hannah Arendt, *Eichmann in Jerusalem: A Report on the Banality of Evil*, London: Penguin, 1964, p. 49.

or the malicious are paradigms of evildoers who we imagine to commit evil intentionally or purposefully. However, much evildoing is not captured by these or other images of antisocial extremes. In fact, evildoing is commonly not even done in recognition of the nature of what one is doing as evil. But such failures of moral understanding are typically not *simply* banal. Indeed, sometimes they are not really banal at all. Instead, we argue, such evildoing is often better described, and explained, in terms of being undertaken in a *moral fog*.[5]

We describe various forms of moral fog ahead, and how it appears both online and in our traditional worlds. Online worlds have created and amplified problems of moral fog, and with this our capacities for moral corruption and evildoing, in a variety of ways. Moreover, the

---

[5] For a short and clear discussion of what Arendt meant by "unthinking," see, Judith Butler, Hannah Arendt's challenge to Adolf Eichmann, *The Guardian*, August 29 2011, available at https://www.theguardian.com/commentisfree/2011/aug/29/hannah-arendt-adolf-eichmann-banality-of-evil (accessed 18 November 2017). See also a collection of interviews with Arendt: *Hannah Arendt: The Last Interview and Other Conversations*, New York, Melville House Publishing, 2013. One of Butler's points (or that comes out of her discussion) is that for Arendt, it is not that evil had become banal in the dictionary sense of ordinary, obvious and unsurprising, but that unthinkingness about the moral status of one's conduct had, under totalitarian regimes, become banal. The account of the moral fog of evil that we go on to develop aims to shed light on what enables this unthinkingness (well beyond the case of totalitarianism). In some cases, we suggest features that may well be banal in the dictionary sense of mundane and unsurprising, such as in cases featuring our learning vulnerabilities, and dependence upon experts, leaders, and mentors. Seen like this, therefore, we may be read as highlighting various ways in which evil really is banal. However, as we argue in Chapter 4, even if our attitudes and/or motives can be described as banal in such cases, our doing evil things from mundane and widely shared motives need not make these cases examples of the banality of evil, at least, not in the sense to which the description of the banality of evil is always applied – namely, to depict *monumental* moral unthinkingness. Many cases are mixed and more nuanced. Thus, one can have fairly banal attitudes and motives, and commit evil, but the problem not be that one is altogether morally unthinking in the sense of *lacking* (or near enough) the capacity to be able to think from the standpoint of someone else. Instead, this capacity has been blindsided or misdirected, for instance, by one's learning vulnerabilities.

nature of values basic to the prosocial, moral life, such as autonomy, intimacy, trust and privacy are transformed online. In particular, the online social revolution has led to the near-total demolition of our abilities to inhabit both of the (generally) quite separate, very different, and often contrasting worlds of public and private life, upon which important features of our basic values depend. As a result, our online-transformed worlds raise some fundamental concerns about the fate of the prosocial, moral life. We begin developing our story about these worries more directly in Chapter 3.

In Chapter 2 we describe the online environment and how many features of the technology and its milieu shape self-expression, communication, and the ways in which people pursue interests and activities. Our discussion here also provides some foundation for our focus in Chapter 3 on the fate of our traditional plural worlds and some of its basic values. In Chapters 4 and 5 we develop our accounts of the moral fog of evil, of moral character and of the prosocial life.

Our investigations into the varied phenomena of evil online, and how they have been enabled by features of our online environments, have unavoidably caused us to look more broadly and deeply at the nature of evildoing and the moral life. We begin our account with some of the cases and major trends of evil online that have led us down these tracks.

1

The Many Faces of Evil Online

Human wickedness is sometimes the product of a sort of conscious leeringly evil intent... But more usually it is the product of a semi-deliberate inattention, in a swooning relationship to time.

Iris Murdoch[1]

1.1 Introduction

In May 2008, hackers bombarded the website of the Epilepsy Foundation of America with hundreds of pictures and links. The site provides advice, news on scientific research and contacts for people who suffer from epilepsy. People who suffer from epileptic seizures have to manage their condition carefully and need regular checkups and medical advice. Epilepsy patients often take precautionary measures to deal with situations where they may be incapacitated and unable to act. Some patients suffer from what is called "photosensitive epilepsy," which means that flickering and flashing images may trigger epileptic seizures. The hackers who attacked the Landover site exploited a security flaw and inserted links to pages with rapidly flashing images. These images were perceived inadvertently by epilepsy patients who were looking for medical information on the website and triggered severe migraines and near-seizure reactions in some site visitors. "They were out to create seizures," said Ken Lowenberg, senior director of web and print publishing for the

[1] Iris Murdoch, *The Black Prince*, Harmondsworth: Penguin, 1973, p. 189.

Evil Online, First Edition. Dean Cocking and Jeroen van den Hoven.

foundation.[2] The hackers did not seem to be interested in money or in control over the victim's computer; they just wanted to create this impact on vulnerable people. "I count this in the same category of teenagers who think it's funny to put a cat in a bag and throw it over a clothesline – they don't realize how cruel it is," said Paul Ferguson, a security researcher at antivirus-software maker Trend Micro Inc.[3]

This is just one of the many examples of evil online that we present in this book. The evils we discuss are not situated on a faraway deserted island, but in another place much closer to home, yet unfamiliar at the same time: our new world of the Internet and social media. Attitudes and conduct may no longer be set in a world of uncharted waters and land, but now they are set in the uncharted territories of our new virtual worlds in cyberspace. This is where our children grow up and teenagers hang out pretty much all day. It is where socialization, moral education, and psychological development takes place. It is the space where young adults live and meet their partners, work, and relax. It is a world that surprises us every day with new inventions and services. And it is a world that is not well-ordered, and that is weakly regulated, monitored, and policed.

This protean cyberdomain is growing and developing at breakneck speed, and it is far from clear who is responsible for what. Facebook and Google earn astronomical amounts of money from the online social and information revolution, but when it comes to taking responsibility for contributing to the social infrastructure of future societies, they are not very active. The responsibility for fake news, the live streaming of suicides, and cascading violence are cases in point. The application of legal principles and moral values in this new territory is deeply problematic. New digital environments constitute a different world, where the voice of traditional moral authorities and the constraints of old social institutions are largely screened from

---

[2] See, http://www.cbc.ca/world/story/2008/05/08/tech-hackers-epilepsy.html (accessed 24 June 2008).

[3] Similar phenomena have occurred victimizing other vulnerable groups. For example, malicious code was released that disabled software that read text aloud from a computer screen for the blind and visually impaired (although the target seemed to be users of illegal copies of the software).

view. Laws often cannot be enforced because of confusion about the nature and status of the phenomena, lack of clarity about jurisdiction, the ineffectiveness of enforcement, and the anonymity of the perpetrators.

It has become clear over the last decade that online contexts have created wonderful opportunities for a vast range of crimes, from cybercrime to child abuse, from cyber-jihad to identity fraud. We are, however, not primarily interested in the online versions of the obvious and straightforward forms of wrongdoing, such as fraud, crime, deception, scams, war, aggression, hate, and violence, with which we are all too familiar from the *offline* history of humanity. These are, by now, all well-known, extensively studied, and are usually referred to by means of prefixing "cyber," "digital," or "online" to the traditional catalogue of crimes and misdemeanors: cyber fraud, digital crimes, identity theft, online deceit and so on. As such, they are not so much novel, surprising, and puzzling as merely recent chapters in a long-lasting arms race between criminals and crime-fighters, between high-tech frauds and cyberforensics.[4] Neither are we primarily interested in the gross depravities that are sometimes seen in serious mental illness, and are now so easily supported and accommodated online. Paraphilias have blossomed online and there is no entry in the DSM classification under that heading without a large online repository of videos, images, and communities associated with it.[5]

Our primary interest is to assess how our new online habitats work against the "better angels" of our nature, and against aspects of our traditional environments and our relationships with others that

[4] As we will point out a few times throughout our discussion, this is not to say that there is "nothing new" so far as these more familiar problems go. See, for example, Chapter 3's discussion of alarmism about online child sex predation, and Section 5.5, "Nothing new under the sun."

[5] See, for example, the early phenomenon of apotemnophilia, in which individuals desire that their arms or legs be amputated, that we present in Chapter 2. Recently, Mary Aiken has also reported cases where peculiar sexual preferences have apparently spread through the Internet. See, Mary Aitken, *The Cyber Effect: A Pioneering Cyberpsychologist Explains How Human Behaviour Changes Online*, London: John Murray (Publishers), 2016.

enable our moral and prosocial capacities. We identify and investigate features of our online worlds that erode empathy and moral character, and that stifle moral and prosocial development.[6] In so doing, we try to understand how young people, among others, are especially vulnerable to becoming victims of the online environments in which they increasingly spend their time. We do not want to take a Luddite or alarmist stance (more on this in Chapters 3 and 5 ahead), or add to the moral panic that sometimes surrounds discussions about social media and the Internet. On the other hand, evil online is an increasingly disturbing phenomenon across a wide range of fronts, and, as is invariably the case with revolutionary technology – and perhaps never more so than with the Internet revolution – our recognition of worries about where we are headed, much less our understanding of these worries, is lagging badly behind. More investigation into the rise of various forms of evil online, and the ways in which our online worlds differ "morally speaking" from our traditional worlds, is well overdue.

We evolved as moral and social beings in our traditional worlds of good old-fashioned causality, contiguity of time and space, unity of action, physical proximity, and face-to-face interaction. In fact, it is in light of these conditions that the evolution of human beings as moral and prosocial creatures (of the kind that we are) makes sense. We have already struggled in the first part of the twentieth century with globalization and the stretching of our moral frameworks and sensibilities beyond the boundaries of our families, clans, cities, regions, and nation states. Now we are well into the twenty-first century, we need to come to grips with our colonization of a digital space that operates under very different conditions, and obeys very different laws.

---

[6] Simon Baron-Cohen has accounted for evil and cruelty in terms of a lack of empathy. Empathy deficiencies and pathologies are accounted for, however, in terms of genetic dispositions and neuroscience. Little attention is given to how relatively ordinary people might lack empathy and commit evil or cruelty in ways that are facilitated by the interplay between human psychology and circumstantial factors. See, Simon Baron-Cohen, *The Science of Evil: On Empathy and the Origins of Cruelty*, New York: Basic Books, 2011.

One thing that is clear is that the Internet and social media disinhibit people and easily escalate conflicts and problems. Once in existence, problems of any nature can cascade like a row of dominoes, and spread like a contagious disease in a large population of interconnected individuals. Chat and comment spaces are regularly filled with abusive language and denigrating remarks. The revolution in speed and access to wonderful ideas has just as effectively been a revolution in the spread of bad ideas. As indicated in our preface, the flourishing of evil online is not confined to the "usual suspects" – those already inclined from deranged, immoral, or criminal intentions. On the contrary, much evil flourishes online (as it long has offline) from the minds of more ordinary and normal people. In developing our account of this territory of evil online, we identify and bring together various characteristics of the online social environment, and of our capacities for evil, and illustrate how the latter may be appeased or summoned depending upon the former.

What we observe and experience at the surface of our online worlds is significantly determined by how the underlying contact network is structured, and by which software and algorithms are at work. All of these ingredients together guide people's conduct online, and make them inclined to do things they could not have (easily) done offline.

A good deal of recent empirical research has shown the ways in which the design of the technology, the mechanisms, circumstances, imperceptible sensory cues, and the design of choice situations are hugely important for the way people behave online. So, for instance, in his book, *The Dark Net,* Jamie Bartlett provides excellent, well-researched descriptions of the spread of some worrying phenomena online, such as assassination markets, suicide and self-harm forums, racism and white supremacy networks, and anorexia and bulimia web sites. He is, however, reluctant to provide a normative analysis of the phenomena encountered online: "it is a series of portraits about how these issues play out at the fringes. I leave it entirely to you to decide what to think it means."[7]

[7] Jamie Bartlett, *The Dark Net: Inside the Digital Underworld*, London: William Heinemann, 2014, p. 7.

Some other scholars in the field have been a little more inclined to provide some moral evaluation.[8] We aim to add to, and move beyond, these very useful though largely descriptive accounts of worrisome cyberphenomena. Not so much by means of more detailed description, but by means of morally relevant explanations, evaluations, and a general framework for ethical understanding of the moral life, and of the conditions under which it is enabled and sustained, or otherwise. As mentioned in our preface, while Hannah Arendt's description of evil as banal has been massively influential, and much evil online may be seen as providing new ways in which evil can flourish and exhibit its banality, we argue that evildoing is often better understood as undertaken in a moral fog. Varieties of this moral fog can be encountered on a deserted island, or a remote and unruly corner of the world, or in an anonymous section of cyberspace with evocative names such as the "Deep Web," "Dark Net," or "Silk Road." It may also be encountered on Facebook, Instagram or Twitter, in a WhatsApp group, or on a chat forum of a high school website. The odds of washing up on the shores of a deserted island are not very high, but all of us are regularly stranded on one of these online places.

There are many kinds of moral fog that apply across cases involving those of otherwise relatively prosocial minds. Thousands of visitors are surrounded by it when visiting the hundreds of websites and forums specializing in self-harm, suicide, anorexia, pedophilia, body dysmorphia, hard drugs, white supremacy, racism, misogyny, anti-Semitism, and terrorism. We identify and discuss various kinds of moral fog throughout this book, from both our online and traditional worlds, and illustrate how thinking of evildoing in this way

[8] See, in particular: Aiken, *op. cit.*; Nancy K. Baym, *Personal Connections in a Digital Age*, Cambridge: Polity Press, 2010; Danah Boyd, *It's Complicated: The Social Lives of Networked Teens*, New Haven, CT: Yale University Press, 2014; Howard Gardner and Katie Davis, *The App Generation. How Today's Youth Navigate Identity, Intimacy, and Imagination in a Digital World,* New Haven, CT: Yale University Press, 2013; and Sherry Turkle, *Alone Together: Why We Expect More From Technology And Less From Each Other*, New York: Basic Books, 2011. All have recently discussed such issues in the contexts of online psychology, socialization, and moral development.

provides broader and deeper explanations of the territory of so-called "banal evil," and takes our understanding of evildoing a long way beyond banality.

1.2 Some Trends and Cases

In the case of the epilepsy hack with which we started this chapter, quite a few questions force themselves upon us. Who were the people who took the trouble to make these posts with the intention of inducing epileptic seizures? They spent many hours applying their computer skills to do so. Why? It wasn't about money or material gain of some sort. Did they really understand the significance of the harm they set out to cause? Or, was it, as the security expert suggested, done just for "fun" without realizing how bad their action was? (Like teens might do in torturing a cat?) The fact that they could not be present to witness the suffering they caused apparently did not make it less "fun." Indeed, it's more likely (perhaps) that not really being there to see the damage inflicted on their victims enabled their lack of moral understanding. Such cases drive us to search for further explanations beyond that given by the seemingly banal description: "it was fun."

Malicious practical jokers on the Internet are called *trolls*; there are many of them around, although they are not usually as bad as this one. Some perpetrators think they are doing the morally right thing, or at least a morally acceptable thing. Often however, application of their moral understanding is somehow suspended in the circumstances, and so they see little need for justification or excuse. The emotional damage and other negative effects that accrue to their victims are often not directly intended, and often not even foreseen.

Much the same is generally true of "catfishing." Catfishing is a form of online identity fraud and deception. The "catfish" is the person who deceives others online. He or she benefits (typically psychologically) by getting attention of some sort, such as romantic attention, or admiration or empathy, from being in a sustained relationship with the victim or the "catfished." Catfish can often sustain a relationship with their victim for a long time without being found out. They typically create an elaborate system of lies and deception, such as about their age, gender, education, health, accomplishments, or socioeconomic status, and may go to extremes to uphold their deceptive schemes and enhancing their fake biographies. A now-famous MTV series, *Catfish*, has unraveled many interesting cases, in emulation of the documentary film, *Catfish*, that gave the phenomenon its name.[9] The original film tells the story of a married woman in a small rural town in Michigan, who presents herself online to a journalist as a young attractive woman, and mother of a girl, a child prodigy in art. The journalist comes to be interested in this very special family and starts to correspond with her and buys paintings by the child prodigy that are shipped to him in New York. Hardly anything in the woman's story turns out to be true, as the journalist finds out when he starts to check the facts and eventually visits her in Michigan. The documentary unravels the elaborate web of lies and deceit. Towards the end of the film her husband responds to the lying and identity fraud of his wife with a story that suggests he neither knew nor wished to know about the second life of his wife, and implies that he even approves of his wife's secret masquerade. He explains that when sailors used to ship live codfish from Alaska to China, the fish would turn mushy in their crates from staying still too long. Then one day, a sailor got the idea of putting catfish in the crates to "keep the cod agile" during the trip. The husband goes on to say that "in life, some people are catfish. They keep things lively." This is a very interesting way of characterizing what in fact amounts to the staging of elaborate lies that cost others significant emotional investment and often money.

The Internet provides many instances of similar redescriptions of actions and behavior that strike others (typically people less embedded in online social worlds) as morally inappropriate or even outrageous. The redescriptions commonly make the acts look harmless, innocent, inadvertent, clueless, funny, a game, even creative or lively – anything but morally wrong. We discuss a number of these cases, and we argue

[9] *Catfish*, Production: Relativity Media, Rogue Pictures. Distribution: Universal Pictures, 2010. See also https://www.psychologytoday.com/blog/more-chemistry/201306/catfish-and-secrets from which we have taken some description of the codfish/catfish story.

that the Internet and the online context provides cyberbullies, catfish, trolls, racists, neo-Nazis, white supremacists, misogynists, terrorists, and other perpetrators of evil online with benign descriptions of their actions that help justify their behavior to themselves and to others. They eventually fool themselves and others into thinking that they are heroic, funny, creative, right, or just interestingly "different."

A notable online trend in which disturbing, even plainly appalling, conduct is often given a light touch and made to look innocent, is the proliferation of so-called prank videos. Indeed, "It's just a prank" is a description of conduct that has become a notable form of moral fog online. One extreme case was provided by the abusive family "Vlogs" (Video blogs) of the Martin family. In one episode, the mother and father aggressively scream and yell at their 9-year-old boy Cody: "What the hell is that? There is ink all over the floor." Cody is crying and clearly very distressed, and sobs that he didn't do it. He is right: he didn't do it, his parents did it. He is the victim of a staged prank. After 3 minutes of yelling at the terrified kid, the parents pull out a bottle of trick ink and say: "It's just a prank, bruh!" This is just one episode in a series of abusive Vlogs on the Martins' YouTube channel, DaddyOFive.

Other nauseating episodes are available in the series. There is one where the father instructs his son to slap his little sister in the face until she cries and one where the father smashes the boy's computer game. Their channel on YouTube made the family $200,000 (or more) annually from the views of their estimated 750,000 subscribers. The case has been brought into the open, the content has been removed, and the parents have lost custody of their children.[10]

You might be inclined to react to this story by thinking that this is just an exception. A spectacularly disconcerting anecdote perhaps, but as rare a form of entertainment as it is extreme. You would be wrong. Many others have engaged in (or supported) this type of abusive content production in pursuit of likes, clicks, and money from advertisements. Vlogging and Live streaming, and especially the

---

[10] We take these facts and description of the case from Rachel Dunphy, "The abusive 'pranks' of YouTube Family Vloggers," *New York* (Magazine), 28 April 2017.

pranking genre, is a global multibillion-dollar business, and millions of people are producing and consuming this type of material. In 2013, YouTube reported that the top ten producers of these prank videos were good for 3.5 billion views. According to Tubular Labs, prank videos accounted for a startling 17.7 billion views in 2015. By 2016 there were an estimated 2.5 million prank videos online on YouTube, created by 1.3 million producers.[11]

According to Caitlin Dewey of the *Washington Post*, "certain pranksters have become increasingly transgressive in a bid to stand out in saturated waters."[12] Roman Atwood is a good example of someone who is pushing the boundaries. He has staged pranks where he pretended to kill his son before the eyes of his wife. He convincingly suggested that a specially prepared car had caught fire with their child inside while the mother was watching. It was viewed 8.6 million times. The video in which he was about to throw his kid off a two-story balcony was viewed 34.7 million times. Atwood described his actions in this way: "I think I am one of the kings of the Internet, of being controversial. I give every website in the world something to talk about – something to cry about. I make the world laugh and cry all at the same time. I'm hard to figure out."[13]

A number of the pranksters enjoy significant notoriety. Ken Duchamp staged a number of fake stabbings and has now, as Dewey puts it, "moved to classier stunts." He is now pretending to have a heart attack in front of girls he has started dating. The stress and anxiety on the part of the girls is usually settled with the words: "relax, relax, it's just a prank." Sam Pepper inappropriately touched young women in public in his prank videos and defended his conduct by saying, "Guys it's OK that I sexually assaulted random women on the street! I didn't mean it. It was a prank… a social experiment." Pepper also deals in more impactful work. He staged a kidnapping of two of his friends by masked men. One of his friends was in the complot, but

---

[11] Geoff Weiss, *Tubefilter*, "The good, the bad and the fake: the rise of YouTube's Prank video genre," 13 April 2016.

[12] Caitlin Dewey, "What 'parody,' 'prank' and other common defenses for dumb internet stunts mean in reality," *Washington Post*, 24 September 2014.

[13] *Ibid.*

the other (the victim) believed that they were being abducted by terrorists. Pepper had them sit in front of a camera and pretended to shoot the friend (who was in on the stunt) in the head. After which he screamed: "It's just a prank…!"[14]

Abusive and violent pranks have been going on online under the name of "happy slapping" for more than twenty years. Unsuspecting victims are attacked, humiliated, or degraded while an accomplice records the assault (commonly with a smartphone) for distribution online. The publication through file-sharing or posting of the event is the rationale for the crime. Most "happy-slappers" are teenagers or young adults. Incidents can be extremely violent, and people have been killed. Often "happy slappers" are encouraged by bystanders, and (just as above) will say they were merely "happy slapping," as if this somehow silences any concern that they may be doing something wrong.[15] For the perpetrators, along with many who consume their product, describing the activity as "just a prank" invokes the relative innocence and fun of fairly harmless pranks, enabling everyone to fool themselves that it is somehow okay.

Tyler Clementi, student at Rutgers University, committed suicide on a September day in 2010. He jumped off the Washington Bridge in New York. As it turned out, he had had sex with a male partner in his room in the university dorm. His intimate moments were recorded live by a webcam secretly installed by his room-mate Dharun Ravi. Ravi had also invited friends via Twitter to watch what was going on in the room in real time and post comments. Ravi later apologized for the "thoughtless, insensitive, immature, stupid, and childish choices…

---

[14] *Ibid.*

[15] "Happy slapping" is known to have started in South London, in particular the London Borough of Lewisham, in a format known as "Slap TV," where a "happy slapping" video would be recorded, and then watched by people like a TV show. Nowadays this is a common form of entertainment, sometimes difficult to tell apart from the Jackass programs where people intentionally risk significant harm to themselves and their friends for a laugh. The perpetrators in these cases often spur each other on, and worries about transgressing moral boundaries (or being part of, or very close to, the "entertainment value" of the broader, including morally awful, happy-slapping scene) sometimes seem to easily get lost in the framing of the conduct as "a joke."

which at no time where motivated by hate, bigotry, prejudice, or the desire to hurt, humiliate, or embarrass anyone."[16] What was Ravi thinking? Did he want to impress his Facebook friends? Did he think it was funny? Did he give any thought to what this would mean in the real life of his roommate? Again the excuse, and lack of explanation, is baffling. How could someone have missed that this is the ultimate humiliation for someone?

The married woman who inspired the description of catfishing, the prankster video producers, and Ravi all seem guilty of fairly self-centered conduct, and misguided about what is funny, interesting, and entertaining, and about what is harmless and innocent. And, of course, they are seriously blind to and wrong about the effects their actions have on others. Their lack of moral imagination and thought about the consequences of their conduct is astounding. A landmark case from the early years of the Internet shows similar characteristics. A Missouri woman created the persona of a 16-year-old boy, Josh Evans, to flirt with and then cruelly spurn her neighbor's daughter, Megan Meier. The 13-year-old girl hanged herself in the wake of the rejection by Josh, communicated to her in the form of a message on her MySpace profile: "The world would be a better place without you." The woman had set-up the "Josh Evans" account after her own daughter had a falling out with Megan.

At the time, the prosecution of the woman sparked a fierce debate about identity online. Authorities initially struggled to find a law which she could be prosecuted for violating, but public outrage over the alleged bullying was intense. Missouri prosecutors were unable to find a state law that had been violated. Federal indictment eventually followed, based on hacking law, alleging that the woman violated MySpace's terms of service when she invented "Josh Evans," and that this amounted to unauthorized network access. US legal experts at the time worried that a successful prosecution could criminalize anyone who posts fake information online. But how could a mother

---

[16] See, http://www.telegraph.co.uk/news/worldnews/northamerica/usa/9299179/Dharun-Ravi-issues-apology-for-his- part-in-Tyler-Clementis-death.html (accessed 12 November 2017).

do such a thing? It required detailed planning, the setting-up and maintaining of an account, and the most callous bullying.[17]

'The Star Wars Kid" is the name of an Internet video which became a viral sensation. Shot in 2002, the then 14-year-old, Ghyslain Raza, was seen practicing with a golf-ball retriever, pretending it was a light saber (as in the *Star Wars* film series). He left the tape without realizing that two of his classmates would find it, convert it to a digital video, and post it online. He inadvertently became an Internet sensation, being dubbed "The Star Wars Kid." Many parodies of the video were created, and his likeness was included in television shows such as "Family Guy" and "Arrested Development." Raza himself, however, suffered immensely due to relentlessly being bullied and taunted by his classmates. His condition deteriorated so much that he stopped attending his Quebec high school and was admitted to a children's psychiatric ward. In an interview he gave (his first) ten years later in 2013, he recalled: "What I saw was mean. It was violent. People were telling me to commit suicide [...] No matter how hard I tried to ignore people telling me to commit suicide, I couldn't help but feel worthless, like my life wasn't worth living."[18] Fortunately, Raza managed to overcome this dark period. As an adult, he earned a law degree from McGill University, and publicly speaks up about his experience in order to help others who have suffered similarly, to "overcome [their] shame."[19]

Nowadays, various forms of cyberbullying, humiliation, harassment, and shaming (more ahead) are widely recognized as significant trends in our online-transformed worlds. The availability of mobile phones at very early ages seems to have triggered and stimulated various forms of cyberbullying. Such problems have become regular business for law enforcement units, agencies, and courtrooms across the globe, and educational programs and

---

[17] This landmark case raised significant awareness about cyberbullying. In particular, see the Megan Meier Foundation and its work on the prevention of bullying and cyberbullying.

[18] http://www.macleans.ca/news/canada/10-years-later-the-star-wars-kid-speaks-out/ (accessed 12 November 2017).

[19] http://gawker.com/star-wars-kid-breaks-silence-says-online-fame-made-h-499800192 (accessed 18 November 2017).

therapeutic instruments to address them have likewise widely appeared. So why the explosion? Some of the main drivers of cyberbullying and harassment can be gleaned from comments that the perpetrators report themselves (in hindsight). Common responses to the question "What made you do this?" are: "Because I could," "I didn't realize...," "I'm anonymous," and "Everyone is doing it." An account representative of many cyberbullies goes like this:

> He thought that it might be fun to act out his fantasies online. He also was convinced that he couldn't get caught. When I asked him why he did it, he said simply, "Because I can." He is a good kid. He's the kind of kid that you'd want your children to be friends with, the one we refer to when we say "Why can't you be more like...?" He never forgets to say please or thank you. He'd never dream of threatening anyone offline. But online he's not a well-mannered honors student. Online he's the tough and violent kid he always fantasized about being. He plays at being someone else. It's the cyberspace version of Dr. Jekyll and Mr. Hyde. And he does it from the safety of his bedroom, after his homework is finished."[20]

Many teenagers get entangled in the Web and lose track of what is real, what is virtual, and where the boundaries between offline and online are. The eighteen-year-old David Sunboli was addicted to violent computer games, which he played for hours, even days, on end, often reversing night and day, and gave himself names such as "God" and "Psycho." He was excluded from online chat groups because of his aggressive behavior. He had been very active online, looking at material on Anders Breivik and high school shootings. Sunboli hacked into the Facebook account of a friend, and posted an invitation to his classmates to come and have a free hamburger at the local McDonalds in a suburb of Munich. When the classmates showed up he embarked upon a killing spree with a semi-automatic hand gun and killed nine children. There was a history of bullying by his classmates, long hours playing violent computer games and long hours in contact with extremist and racist white supremacy content. David lost his orientation in a confusing and

---

[20] See, http://stopcyberbullying.org/doc/because_i_can.doc (accessed 13 October 2017).

fogged up moral social world. The online environment was part of his problem, and also part of his solution.

In August 2012, a heavily intoxicated teenage girl was sexually assaulted by high school football players after passing out at a party in Steubenville Ohio. She was dragged around and sexually assaulted many times. Bystanders took pictures, made videos with their cellphones and shared them via Instagram, Facebook, Twitter, and text messaging. One tweet read: "Song of the night is definitely 'Rape Me' by Nirvana." The latter was meant as a joke. In a toxic mixture of alcohol, drugs, social media, smartphones, and fraternity "partying," the most horrible things happened, yet were given a relatively light touch by soshed."[21]

Many people, often parents and educators, are understandably worried about these and similar stories. They fear that children and young people may become victims, and they fear that somehow they may also become perpetrators. Is it just the unfamiliarity with a new medium and new technology? Or is there something special about the online environment that keeps the perpetrators from understanding the moral nature of their actions and what the consequences for others could be? Are there properties of the online environment that encourage or facilitate this type of behavior, or will (perhaps, in any case) these evils subside once we all have become more accustomed to social media and the online environment and how to navigate it?

We describe most of our cases in some detail to show how the digital technology of the online world may shape our moral lives, our moral thinking, feeling and sensibilities. There are many more stories and cases of morally worrying behavior that might be used to draw attention to the downsides of the Internet and its features that might enable such problems. We discuss many of the latter features in the chapter ahead. A large number of the cases we discuss throughout this book are unique to the online world, or uniquely enabled by the online environment. All of the cases involve some significant derailing and deformity of moral and prosocial identity. On the basis of these and

[21] For this and other cases of young people running amok online, see, Carrie James, *Disconnected: Youth, New Media and the Ethics Gap*, Cambridge, MA., MIT Press, 2014.

other cases we argue that there is a special sort of confusion at work – what we refer to as "moral fog" – that envelops the online world and brings forms of moral disorientation that facilitates evildoing.

This applies especially to young people who are growing up, and being introduced to the meaning and importance of moral values, and to the needs and interests of other human beings. A large part of socialization and moral education now takes place in digital environments not at all designed with the education of morally sensitive, pro-social future citizens in mind. This is in stark contrast to the history of our cultures and civilizations, which (with varying degrees of success) have invariably concerned themselves with the design of cultural, social, and institutional environments that facilitated the moral development (by their lights) of their future citizens.

Moral fog can also form a danger to oneself. Many children, for example, fall under the spell of eating disorders: anorexia, bulimia, and most recently "orthorexia." In all of these cases, their disorders are a threat to themselves rather than to others.[22] Anorexia is an eating disorder prevalent among girls in their puberty and adolescence which consists in compulsive fasting and extreme dieting. It may eventually result in life-threatening malnourishment and death. One in every hundred girls in the Western world suffers from mild or severe forms of anorexia. It is, of course, very difficult to treat anorexia precisely because those who suffer from it are victims of distorted views of their own body. Ideals of beauty and fashion dictate to young girls in a vulnerable period of their identity formation that they should have slim, even skinny, figures, and preach extreme ideas about health. Fashion models seem thinner every year, and being skinny is glorified and seen as reflecting an admirable lifestyle. Although anorexic girls have Body Mass Indexes which are agreed by medical specialists to be unhealthy, and even dangerously low given their age, height and physical constitution, they compulsively keep seeing themselves as too fat.

[22] One exception would be the impact one's conduct has in influencing others to take up self-destruction. In the anorexia case this is a notable impact since, as in many other case types, the online community significantly reinforces self-destructive behaviors.

The Internet has significantly facilitated the coming together of anorexic girls in online communities. These so-called "pro-ana sites" glorify anorexia. What are the people behind these sites thinking? Don't they realize they are endangering the lives of vulnerable teenagers? The condition is portrayed on these sites as an intentionally chosen way of life which is valuable and deserves respect – not as a morbid interest in losing weight and being unhealthily skinny. The sites provide tips on how to lose weight and burn calories, how to fast and starve, and how to hide all of this from parents. You can have a normal meal with the family, but throw up afterwards. In order to hide this from members of the family, it is advised to do so while having a shower, because the noise of vomiting is then masked by the noise of the shower. The sites also encourage people to harden themselves against the exhortations of their caretakers and parents to eat.

A website dedicated to the promotion of anorexia, allegedly the largest of its kind, has many postings by young girls who want to lose weight. A girl writes the following: "Okay, so today was going so well … I got to 3pm with only 200 cals, then I was practically forced to eat cake and stuff so as not to cause suspicion. Oh my God I'm at 800 cals. I hate this." Yet another posting in the early afternoon, by the same girl: "So far, I have had a cup of tea, hoping to keep it that way." Another girl bemoans the arrival of her period: "I feel so bloated, water weight has added a devastating 1lb to 3lb." Girls post pictures of themselves, bones protruding from skin, looking like famine victims. With their skinny bodies they adopt the sexy poses of fashion models. Yet they claim to feel good, as one teen wrote on the website: "Yesterday I skipped dinner … so I had about 250 calories. I'm gaining control. Yes." And so it goes on. These are the kind of websites which had been visited regularly by Imogen D'Arcy, a 13-year-old girl from Leeds who hanged herself in despair because she thought that she was too "fat" and "ugly." In the weeks before her death her self-destructive obsession with her own body image was fueled by scouring the Internet for information on anorexia and suicide.[23]

[23] For discussion of the case, see, e.g., http://www.telegraph.co.uk/news/uknews/3525738/Perfectionist-schoolgirl-hanged-herself-while-worried-about-appearance.html (accessed 12 November 2017).

Orthorexia Nervosa[24] is an eating disorder which is essentially an obsession with *healthy* food. This is rapidly becoming a large problem as a result of its contagious spread on social media: "Networks such as Facebook and Instagram are a haven for social comparison, and it is extremely easy for people, in particular adolescents, to get caught in negatively comparing themselves to others, based on highly crafted images… With the constant barrage of images, women and men are daily, and even hourly, reminded of how they are falling short next to these unrealistic standards."[25] This is one of the reasons why orthorexia has been referred to as the digital-age eating disorder.

On the basis of in-depth interviews and study of online communities, Bartlett observes: "Every day, thousands of people from all over the world visit the sprawling networks of forums, blogs, and websites dedicated to various types of self-harm: anorexia, self-mutilation, suicide."[26] There are hundreds of suicide forums that welcome their visitors with "Sorry you're here." An overview of the research indicates that there are circa 500 pro anorexia sites, and roughly the same number of "pro-cutting and suicide sites." Bartlett reports, for example, how the sites provide practical advice on how to cut oneself if parents limit the number of cutting tools in the house, and concludes: "Tips and tricks are arguably the most harmful and destructive parts of these subcultures, transforming what might be vague, ill-thought out plans into a concrete set of instructions."[27]

Sometimes people gather to watch live suicide attempts. The contagiousness of these type of behaviors are, by now, well-known, researched and validated. People support each other, but also encourage each other's destructive behavior: "By wrapping up negative behavior in an ordinary, positive, and romantic way – by surrounding each user

---

[24] http://www.heraldsun.com.au/news/national/orthorexia-why-the-too-clean-diet-spreadby-social-media-is-pure-hell/news-story/0c7e5bc3ca2ea7970a882e09220646d0 (accessed 12 November 2017).

[25] *Ibid.*

[26] *Op. cit.*, p. 194

[27] *Op. cit.*, p. 206

with peer support – it insidiously makes an illness feel like a culture, a life style choice, something to be embraced."[28]

The early days of the Internet gave us a striking example of how free-wheeling from moral realities online contagion can be, with the case of "Nevada-tan," the name used to describe an 11-year-old Japanese schoolgirl who was charged with murdering her classmate.[29] The name derives from the fact that in a school photo she can be seen to wear a University of Nevada sweater, and "tan" is an honorific suffix in Japanese.

"Girl A," as she is referred to in the police reports, had retreated into an online fantasy world of horror and death, collecting "flash" horror movies on a website she had started, visiting violent sites and constantly searching for bloodier ones, and appealing to others to join her by commencing her own blog containing many gruesome stories… and some cooking recipes. The murder occurred in 2004 at an elementary school and involved slitting her friend's throat and arms with a retractable knife after the friend had made hurtful and humiliating remarks about her during exchanges in Internet chat rooms.

As a result Japanese media were led to identify some of the dangers of the Internet. "We must make children understand even more the basic importance of life," the *Yomiuri* newspaper said in an editorial. "What children need most is to be able to piece together real things and real experiences," wrote Hisashi Sonoda, an Internet crime expert at Konan University.[30] The *Tokyo Shimbun*, a major metropolitan newspaper, also observed: "Over a computer… you can't see the person's face, so it's easier to use increasingly violent language. If that's the case, it's an incident that reflects a pathology of

---

[28] *Op. cit.*, p. 217

[29] Most of our description of the case is taken from www.tvwiki.tv/wiki/Nevada-tan (accessed 12 November 2017). See also, https://en.wikipedia.org/wiki/Sasebo_slashing (accessed 12 November 2017).

[30] Cited and translated by the BBC, http://news.bbc.co.uk/2/hi/asia-pacific/3772737.stm (accessed 12 November 2017).

society in the age of the Internet."[31] Nevertheless Girl A soon became an Internet sensation. Japanese web communities Futaba Channel and 2channel "adopted" her. Artists on 2channel turned Girl A into a cute anime character dubbed "Nevada-tan." Her personal website became very popular, and when it was taken down, mirror sites were put up. Copies of her artwork circulated on the web, and others copied her stuff. Fan songs, such as "Cutie NeVaDa" appeared.[32] Nevada Tan is also the name of a German Rock band that rose to significant popularity with songs like "No one hears you."[33]

A very different kind of case, also evident from the early days and now among the more widely recognized examples of how evil can get enormous traction online, is online pedophilia. In one case, a decade ago, two suspected pedophiles went on trial in northern France accused of planning to kidnap, rape and torture a little girl, and boasting of their plans on the Internet. Christian Cadart, a 49-year-old telecommunication technician from the northern Rouen region, and Herve Limbour, 41, a painter–decorator from the Riviera city of Nice, were arrested in May, 2007, after a tip from a fellow web user. According to the prosecution, the two men plotted in detail, over the Internet messaging service MSN, how they would kidnap, sexually torture and possibly kill a child. Cadart, who went by the pseudonym "Herrio," was arrested as he showed an undercover officer the disused electric power transformer where he said he planned to sequester his victim. His alleged accomplice, Limbour, who called himself "Diablo," was arrested after making telephone calls describing sexual assaults on girls in his home town. The men had met in a pedophile chat forum and had been reinforcing one another's sexual fantasies about

---

[31] Cited and translated by Fox News, http://www.foxnews.com/story/2004/06/03/girl-says-internet-tv-led-her-to-slay-friend.html (accessed 12 November 2017).

[32] In June 2005, the online store that sold the University of Nevada hooded sweatshirt reported it to be their best-selling item (this was reported in the site's online statistics, and, a few weeks later, the University temporarily removed the sweatshirt from their catalog).

[33] On the German rock band, see, for instance, https://en.wikipedia.org/wiki/Panik_(band) (accessed 12 November 2017).

young girls for a long time, along with kidnap-planning on MSN. Both insisted, however, that the kidnap plans were a mere fantasy never intended to be carried out. They admitted that everything was coherent and feasible, but claimed they never really thought about putting it into practice. As they described it, they were in a state of "delirium" online. The court disagreed and the men were sentenced to ten years' imprisonment.[34]

The grooming of young people for sexual purposes is widespread online. The act of grooming a child or young person sexually often includes ordinary activities, not illegal or immoral in themselves, that later leads to sexual contact. Typically, this is done to gain the child or young person's trust, as well as the trust of those responsible for their wellbeing. Sex abusers of children and young people find the Internet a very supportive environment for their activities – for instance, due to the anonymity of the medium. Thus, for example, online abusers often pose as children in order to facilitate arrangements to meet with their victims in person. Online worlds have also provided atypical access for sexual predators to their victims in other ways. So, for instance, predators have been able to use Trojan horses, malicious software that allows them to hijack the webcam of their victim, and generate images which the predator can then use for themselves, or to blackmail their victim, say, by threatening to post the images so they will go viral on the web. Grooming and sex predation has flourished online. As with cyberbullying and harassment, many studies have now been carried out, many laws enacted, and many enforcement agencies and educational programs set up around the world to address the phenomena directly.

Revenge porn is another significant and well-known online trend. This is a form of sexual abuse that involves the distribution of nude/sexually explicit photos and/or videos of an individual without their consent. The general term for making available personal documents without a person's consent is "doxing." Revenge porn is a special case of doxing, sometimes called cyber-rape or non-consensual pornography,

[34] See, www.lexpress.fr/infos/pers/christian-cadart.html (accessed 20 June 2017).

and is usually posted by a scorned ex-lover or friend in order to seek revenge after a relationship has gone sour. The explicit photos and videos are often posted using the victim's full name, address, email, telephone, links to their social media profiles, and sometimes even links to their employers. Certain sites such as "Is Anyone Up" run by Hunter Moore, have played a crucial role in hosting revenge porn and adding information identifying the victim and connecting them to the material posted. As a result, victims are often harassed by strangers, cyberstalked, sent unsolicited emails and phone calls, and receive unwanted visitors at their home.

Victims of revenge porn have even lost their jobs after their photos or videos were posted online. In turn, many have then found it difficult to get a new job, since prospective employers are easily directed to the photographs or videos. Many find themselves publicly ridiculed or condemned, and they are often inclined to blame themselves, thinking that they should not have made the photographs or videos in the first place. Several activists are fighting for new laws that criminalize the publication of private material without explicit consent. At the forefront has been Charlotte Laws, an activist who started a legal fight against Hunter Moore, owner of the "Is Anyone Up" website, after her daughter's topless photo was uploaded there. The growth of revenge porn has also led to prenuptial social media agreements about the use of any nude or sexual material.

Online shaming is now a widely recognized (and increasingly opposed) online trend. It is a form of digital vigilantism, where social media and websites are used in order to expose and possibly punish people or businesses who are considered to have behaved in an immoral, cruel, or discriminatory fashion. The shaming can take many forms, including revealing information about the person's identity, calls to their employer to fire them, disparaging tweets, and even death threats. At its best, online shaming can be used as a way to shed light on systemic injustices (consider, for example, the Twitter account @EverydaySexism which documents women's experiences worldwide with sexist behavior and harassment). At its worst, online shaming can turn into a form of digital witch-hunting, where reputations are destroyed, and victims are slandered.

Jon Ronson has examined several cases of people who have been shamed online, and whose lives, as a result, have been irrevocably changed.[35] He notes that the original motives behind online shaming can be "pure": we notice someone behaving in an immoral way, and we seek to make clear to this person, and perhaps generally, that this conduct will not be tolerated. However, even in cases where there is some righteous outrage to be had, such acts of online vigilantism often cascade into massively unjustified consequences, such as hate campaigns and death threats, causing extreme and long-lasting psychological damage to their victims.

One of the cases Ronson discusses is that of Lindsey Stone, a young woman in her twenties. Stone, who used to work in a foundation for learning disabilities, had a tradition of making rather crass jokes, such as taking photographs with her friend, "smoking in front of a no-smoking sign or posing in front of statues, mimicking the pose." As she says: "We took dumb pictures all the time."[36] On a day when she visited the Arlington Military Cemetery, she and her friend took what they thought was a funny picture of her posing in front of a "Silence and Respect" sign. Stone pretended to yell and flip her middle finger towards the sign. The photo was posted by her friend on Facebook. However, the privacy settings were set to public, so anyone was able to find the photograph. Soon enough (and sure enough), people started reacting to the picture, accusing Stone of disrespecting the Armed Forces, the veterans, and the soldiers who gave their lives. A Facebook group demanding her firing was started, more than 30,000 Facebook users joined, and another 3,000 signed a petition demanding that she be sacked.[37] The foundation for which she was working fired her a few days later.

This marked the beginning of a terrible period for Stone. She became depressed and for a year found it difficult to leave her house.

---

[35] Jon Ronson, *So You've Been Publicly Shamed?* London: Picador (Pan Macmillan), 2015.

[36] http://www.theguardian.com/technology/2015/feb/21/internet-shaming-lindsey-stone-jon-ronson (accessed 12 November 2017).

[37] http://gawker.com/5962796/happy-now-good-employee-lindsey-stone-fired-over-facebook-photo (accessed 12 November 2017).

She became obsessed with reading everything that was posted online about her, and no one would reply to her work applications. Eventually, she did find employment in caring for the autistic children of a family. She remained, however, constantly terrified that her new employers would find out about the photograph, and the extraordinary online shaming that had ensued. It also became very difficult for her to meet new people: "It really impacts the way you view the world. Since it happened, I haven't tried to date anybody. How much do you let a new person into your life? Do they already know?"[38]

A more recent example is the case of Walter Palmer, an American dentist. He caused a worldwide uproar when it became known that he had killed a beloved lion called Cecil during a safari trip in Zimbabwe. Cecil was a part of a lion pride that lived in Hwange National Park in Zimbabwe. Cecil wore a GPS collar, and his whereabouts were monitored by a team of researchers. He was allegedly lured away from the protected area of the park, where Parker shot and wounded him with an arrow. On July 1 2015, about 40 hours after he had been shot by the arrow, Cecil was shot dead with a rifle, decapitated and skinned.

When Palmer was identified as the hunter who killed Cecil, a tidal wave of negative reactions followed. People were calling for his arrest, for a boycott of his dental practice, and even for his death. His home and work addresses were revealed, and protesters started gathering outside his private dental practice, holding signs with slogans such as "Punish Palmer" and "Stop Trophy Hunting." The words "Lion Killer" were spray-painted on the garage door of his vacation house.[39] Even celebrities, and people like Jane Goodall, the world-famous primatologist, expressed their anger and disgust over Cecil's killing.[40] Palmer maintained that he had paid for and obtained a license which allowed him to hunt lions, that he trusted the knowledge of his guides, and that he did not know that the lion he killed belonged in a

---

[38] https://www.theguardian.com/technology/2015/feb/21/internet-shaming-lindsey-stone-jon-ronson (accessed 12 November 2017).

[39] https://www.cbsnews.com/news/cecil-the-lion-vandals-attack-vacation-home-of-dentist-who-killed-lion/ (accessed 12 November 2017).

[40] See, http://qz.com/467277/jane-goodall-on-cecil-the-lions-death-i-have-no-words-to-express-my-repugnance/ (accessed 12 November 2017).

protected national park. Had he known this, he said, he would not have killed Cecil.[41] Finally, the Zimbabwean authorities decided on October 2015 that there was no basis to press charges against Palmer, and he would be allowed to come back to Zimbabwe – though as a tourist, not a hunter.[42]

Online shaming is global and everlasting for the victim; it is also easily open for the rest of us to join in. Monica Lewinsky (also interviewed by Ronson) is another who, like Lindsay Stone, had their identity and ability to relate to others utterly swamped by online shaming. Like many others who are shamed and bullied online, who these people were and who they could be was reduced to a particular episode. An episode, which plainly, in itself, did not warrant the near all-encompassing and ongoing reduction and devastation of their lives.[43]

One of the more spectacular and widely recognized ways in which our online-transformed worlds have enabled evil has been the growth of terrorism, and radicalization to terror. In his contemporary history of home-grown terrorism in the United States, Peter Bergen has analyzed hundreds of young people (both Christian and Muslim) who have been led astray in the labyrinth of extremist jihadist online content.[44] Half of the 330 militants that Bergen researched were very active online. One story, representative of many, exemplifies a number of the features to which we have drawn attention. It is the story of Zac Chesser, an American high school student. Chesser was a well-rounded, good student who had no problems with math, Latin, or Japanese, and who rowed and played football. His parents were successful college-educated professionals – a lawyer and an economist.

[41] http://www.bbc.co.uk/news/world-africa-34508269 (accessed 12 November 2017).

[42] http://www.bbc.co.uk/news/world-africa-34508269 (accessed 12 November 2017).

[43] Lewinsky is now an active campaigner against online bullying. For the Ronson interview see, https://www.theguardian.com/technology/2016/apr/16/monica-lewinsky-shame-sticks-like-tar-jon-ronson (accessed 18 November 2017).

[44] Peter Bergen, *Homegrown United States of Jihad: Investigating America's Homegrown Terrorists*, New York: Crown Publishers, 2016.

His grandfather was a retired army colonel who went to West Point and served in Vietnam. Over a period of a couple of years Chesser transformed from a nice high school kid into a young man who posted a message on a militant jihadi website. His message was a detailed plan on how to "desensitize Federal agents" by planting a number of fake bombs before planting real bombs; then, as he put it, "Boom! No more *kuffar*" (non-believers).[45]

It all started when he fell in love with a Muslim girl, a daughter of Somali immigrants.[46] He started to look into Muslim culture and religion. Gradually his lifestyle changed as he increasingly spent time hanging out with Muslim friends and consuming jihadist propaganda online. He joined groups that were spreading the ideas of Bin Laden and Awlaki. Within a year he developed into a bearded, extremist Muslim, one of the hubs in a virtual Holy War. He had rapidly built a significant reputation in a cybercommunity of jihadis, creating websites, online magazines, blogs, and password-protected online forums that spread extremist jihadist content. As Chesser himself understood: "The Internet led to a rapid rise in Jihadism as it offered up a podium…."[47] In his book on terrorism and the Internet, Gabriel Weimann concluded that by 2006 religious Muslim extremism had increased its online basis in a decade from a dozen to more than 5000 websites. [48] Many of the subjects he examined admitted that pro-jihad online videos and blogs played a very important role in their conversion and radicalization. Chesser, for instance, told a special agent that he was watching online videos "almost obsessively."[49]

In the online community of self-radicalized jihadism, Chesser was able to significantly advance his reputation by making good use of his

---

[45] See Bergen's description of the Chesser case, *Ibid.*, pp. 131–136.

[46] Of course, our intimate relations have, in various ways, long been more than sufficient to send us astray. Obviously we are highlighting here the phenomenal additional and distinctive traction that the Internet provides.

[47] Bergen, *op. cit.*, p. 136.

[48] Gabriel Weimann, *Terror on the Internet: The New Arena, The New Challenges*, Washington, DC: United States Institute of Peace Press, 2006.

[49] Bergen, *op. cit.*, p. 147.

computer skills. He had set up three YouTube channels[50], and launched the idea of an "open source jihad," envisaging easy access to sources that provide information about making bombs and weapons, tactics, and information on counterterrorism and screening policies by government agencies. He was carefully tracking visits to his site, and was proud that counterterrorism officials were consulting with him. In 2010, he boasted:

> both my YouTube page and several others have seen more traffic than in all of 2009… The growth of my page and some others I pay attention to is looking to hit a rate that would produce more than 1,000,000 views per year. There are currently no Jihadi YouTube pages with even that many total views.[51]

As Bergen observed: "In his own mind Chesser was the world's foremost Internet holy warrior…"[52] He had certainly become thoroughly confused in the maelstrom of his sudden notoriety. He daydreamed about joining the real holy war, joining Al Shabaab and travelling to Somali, to see action. He planned, for instance, to travel to Uganda with his orthodox Muslim wife. She was 9 months pregnant at the time. Half a year later he thought he could fly to Uganda, from there to Kenya and on to Somalia, with the last leg in a speedboat. To top it off he planned to fly from New York's JFK airport (where he was stopped at security, because he was by that time on a no-fly list) to Uganda with his 7-month-old son, go by foot to Kenya, and then continue their walk into Somalia.

Again (as we suggested earlier in regard to extreme pranks), you might agree that such specific cases depict some terrible corruption, and you might even agree that the online world seems implicated. However, you might well also think that the online worlds of Chesser and the like are very rare, and so a very small part of online activity. And so you might well think that such cases do not really present much of an indictment against life in our online-transformed worlds.

---

[50] Bergen, *op. cit.*, p.145

[51] Bergen, *op. cit.*, pp. 149–150.

[52] Bergen, *op. cit.*, p. 157.

Again, none the less, you would be wrong. Sites promoting terror are nothing like marginal dark alleys. As, for example, Bartlett reports, the FBI estimates that one of the sites Chesser was involved in belonged to the 1% of sites on the Web that generated the most traffic.

The organization and dynamics of the opposing camp of anti-Muslim activists exhibits the very same features, as white supremacists and white pride advocates organize themselves online. Bartlett describes how the Internet plays a central role in spreading ideas about white supremacy, white pride and neo-Nazism. The website Stormfront.org has hundreds of thousands of members who together have posted ten million messages. In 2013, The Simon Wiesenthal Center estimated that there were 20,000 active hate websites (and rising). The typical modern nationalist and potential radicalized member is, according to Bartlett's profile: "young, time rich, technologically literate – able to quickly and easily connect virtually to like-minded people around the world."[53]

Bartlett held interviews with many nationalist and right-wing enthusiasts, and describes how social media played a crucial role in the development and dissemination of the extremist ideas of Anders Breivik. Lone wolves like Breivik, who do not necessarily prepare their heinous crimes with others, still benefit from virtual communities. They reach out to like-minded people and create environments that echo their views. In this way they receive positive feedback, which reinforces their ideas. Breivik intentionally created a vast network of thousands of Facebook friends among right-wing groups, collected thousands of high quality e-mail addresses, suggested that Wikipedia could be subtly infiltrated to plant his ideas, and practiced his shooting skills by playing the online shooting game *Call of Duty.*

Bartlett's study of small groups of extreme nationalists and their anti-fascist opponents illustrates how the same picture holds everywhere:

> [T]he same dynamic allows hundreds of small often closed communities and individuals to surround themselves with information and people that corroborate their world view, and gives violent racists

[53] *Op. cit.*, p. 52

and xenophobes a platform on which to spread their message quickly and effectively.[54]

After having been exposed to racist, white supremacist, and neo-Nazi content and communities online, Dylann Storm Roof, a 21-year-old from South Carolina, confessed to killing nine people at a historic black church in Charleston. He hoped it would start a race war. Roof created a website called "The Last Rhodesian," a reference to the white-ruled African country which fought a civil war against black majority rule before it became Zimbabwe. The website features a manifesto in which Roof wrote how he had been radicalized via the Internet. He said he had researched "black on white violence," which took him to the website of South Carolina-based hate group the Council of Conservative Citizens (formerly the White Citizens' Council). "N****** are stupid and violent," Roof wrote, and further:

> I chose Charleston because it is the most historic city in my state, and at one time had the highest ratio of blacks to whites in the country… We have no skinheads, no real KKK, no one doing anything but talking on the Internet. Well someone has to have the bravery to take it to the real world, and I guess that has to be me.[55]

One of the most broad and transformational impacts of the Internet has been upon the social lives and psychological development of young people. Recently, based on the findings of a large research project ("Project Zero"), Howard Gardner and Katie Davis have reported on the influence of social media upon the education and psychological development of children, teenagers and young adults.[56] They indicate how 3 million apps (and rising) available to the young can either increase their imagination and options, or have the opposite effect by making them dependent upon the technology. It is clear from their findings that young people think of the world as an

---

[54] *Op. cit.*, p. 70.

[55] https://www.thedailybeast.com/dylann-roofs-racist-manifesto-is-chilling (accessed 12 November 2017).

[56] Gardner and Davis, *The App Generation*, *op. cit.*

ensemble of online tools and platforms, an "app milieu," and they suggest that there are some distinctive differences between the app generation, and previous generations.[57] Indeed, they say: "generations may be defined by their dominant technologies, with the length of a generation dependent on the longevity of a particular technological innovation."[58] In the spirit of the slogan, "The medium is the message," technology is no mere tool. Instead, it can re-create human psychology.

Gardner and Davis also find that young people do not generally distinguish between their online and offline selves, that there is considerable evidence young people take care to present a "socially desirable, polished self, online," and that:

> Features such as asynchronicity and anonymity (or at least the feeling of anonymity) allow young people to craft strategic self-presentations by deciding what information to highlight, downplay, exaggerate, or leave out entirely.[59]

They sketch a picture of constant networked individualism, networked publics and constant (micro) performance that is propelled by the metrics of likes, endorsements, visits, and followers. All of this, they say, can render individuals insecure due to a lack of self-knowledge, and a lack of any robust sense of themselves.[60] Indeed, there is some evidence that the more prominent is someone's online presence, the weaker is their sense of self.[61] Further still, they say many social scientists observe a "positive connection between narcissism and on-line behavior." This is especially evident in the very high

[57] *Ibid.*, p. 11.
[58] *Ibid.*, p. 21. And, as they correctly remark: "Most of what we accomplish online is the result of procedures that have been created by others…," p. 24.
[59] *Ibid.*, p. 63. And also: "Digital media give youth the time and tools to craft an attractive identity, as well as an audience to view and respond to it," p. 70. We analyze the transformation of self-presentation and social communication online, and its impact upon key aspects of our basic values, in detail in Chapter 3.
[60] *Ibid.*, p. 75.
[61] *Ibid.*, p. 86.

levels of self-promoting content found in social activity on sites such as Facebook, and in "tweeting." In offline conversation, people talk about themselves 40% of the time. Online this doubles to 80% of the time.[62]

Gardner and Davis (along with Turkle[63]) paint a fairly bleak picture of the online social milieu. They see a lot of connectivity but no real connections. Instant intimacy, or "instamacy": a pick and choose mentality, distracted by gadgets and constant availability, interruptions, and the checking of e-mail and messages. A milieu marked by the coarsening of language, and of the logic of face-to-face contact (in order to make it look as if you are looking someone in the eyes, you have to look into the camera – not into their eyes). They discuss reports in dropping levels of empathy in youth, and ask: "Could viewing the world through our apps be hurting our ability to view the world through another's eyes?"[64] They observe how the online environment allows shortcuts and enables us to bypass time-consuming face-to-face contact, but that this convenience comes at a cost. Risks of social interaction are diminished, connectivity replaces richer connections. So while we may no longer put ourselves "on the line" so much, we also do not truly connect with others and so, Gardner and Davis worry, "we can't put ourselves in their shoes."[65] In our analysis of our online-transformed social worlds in Chapter 3, we aim to show how various aspects of our basic values are being undermined and perverted by the kinds of self-presentation and communication enabled and favored by the design of these worlds.

---

[62] *Ibid.*, p. 76. They also refer to other research that reports increasing moodiness, restlessness, worry, sadness, and feelings of isolation in this context. See, p. 77.

[63] Turkle, *Alone Together*, *op. cit.*

[64] *Ibid.*, p. 112.

[65] *Ibid.*, p. 119. And, also: "We realized early on that aspects of the new media – their speed, their public nature, the ease of accessing, transferring, and transforming information, the possibilities for anonymity or for multiple identities – were creating a virtual Wild West. Ethical issues… were necessarily coming up for re-examination and perhaps for reconceptualization," p. 170.

The list of trends and cases we have discussed, can, unfortunately, be built upon endlessly with examples from newspapers every day, all over the world. They all indicate how the design and nature of communication contexts, and many kinds of related environmental cues, impact in ways that play an important role in determining antisocial behavior, and in corrupting the moral life. In describing our trends and cases we have noted some specific features of our online environments that seem important in enabling the evils we have canvassed, such as isolation, connection, contagion, positionality, and anonymity. We now turn our focus more directly to describe these and many other features of our online-transformed worlds, and to illustrate how they play a crucial role in shaping our lives, including in ways conducive to evil.

2

Our Online Environment

We shape our buildings, and afterwards, our buildings shape us
Sir Winston Churchill[1]

2.1 Introduction

The World Wide Web now significantly defines the way that we lead our lives. It frames and guides a lifeworld of experiences, thoughts, intentions, ambitions, plans, pastimes, feelings, and emotions. Many of us have our own corner in cyberspace, a Facebook account, a Twitter account, a favorite website, or even a personal website from which we venture out and connect to others. We now live together with our Facebook accounts, WhatsApp, Snapchat, Flicker, Pinterest, and YouTube, and the circa 7 million Apps that are made for our smartphones. We don't need to sit behind a desk to go online, we use tablets, laptops, and smartphones. The online world is now accessed for around 60% of the time via mobile smart devices. The penetration of cheap mobile telephones with Internet access will no doubt reach near-full coverage on the world population in the remainder of this century. There are already as many smartphones as there are people. Smart devices of all sorts are starting to form an "Internet of Things" that will gradually blend into one amalgamated "Internet of Everything."

[1] Sir Winston Churchill, (1874–1965), British Prime Minister (1940–1945 and 1951–1955). This famous quote about architecture comes from a speech to the British House of Commons in October 1943.

Evil Online, First Edition. Dean Cocking and Jeroen van den Hoven.

It all started with four connected computers a few decades ago. There are now 2.5 billion of them. This makes the Internet the largest manmade artefact. There are a staggering 10 to the power of 12 webpages (a million million). Every minute there are around a million YouTube views, Google searches and Facebook posts. Enormous amounts of data are accumulating at staggering speed in the databases of the big five companies that are more or less running our digital society from their platforms and services.

Of all the information humans have ever produced until now – from Egyptian papyri and Sumerian clay tablets onwards – 90 % of it has been produced in the last 24 months. We are moving to an amount of information produced annually measured in zettabytes,[2] which is the equivalent of a stack of books twenty times the distance from earth to Pluto, or 250 billion movies in HD video. Every minute more services and products, from both the public and private sector, are offered on online platforms (such as, YouTube, Facebook, App stores, and ITunes). As a result, we spend a rapidly increasing amount of time online – especially the younger generations, those who were "born digitally." By 2008, children at the age of ten in the US and Europe were spending three hours per day (on average) in front of a computer with an Internet connection. British teenagers now spend more than nine hours a day "digitally engaged"; the average British teenager, for example, spends 1 hour 40 minutes a day on social media websites such as Facebook and Twitter, and approximately the same amount of time on making and editing videos at home. In addition, they spend 15 minutes a day taking selfies to send to their friends or post online.[3]

The real world has in large part migrated to the online world. Children born in the twenty-first century chat with friends, date, play online games, do their homework, search and share music, photos

---

[2] A zettabyte is 10^{21} bytes.

[3] For the latter figures regarding teens, see, http://www.dailymail.co.uk/news/article-3514671/Teenagers-spend-nine-hours-day-addicted-Facebook-Twitter-laptops-smartphones.html (accessed 13 November 2017).

and videos, make reservations, and buy and order online. Gerry Carroll, author of a study on the use of the Internet and social media by teenagers in the UK, said: "For this generation, there is an app for everything and, if one doesn't exist, a growing number are acquiring the coding skills to build their own."[4] Children grow up with the Internet and its myriad applications in the same way they grew up (only) thirty years ago with Crayola crayons and Disney.

Features of the Internet, and characteristics of the way it is utilized, are important for understanding the dynamics of many morally problematic episodes of life online, such as those we described in our first chapter (and those we will describe in our next). We use the expressions, "our online lifeworlds," "our online-transformed worlds," and "our online environment," as umbrella terms to capture and refer to the realm of experience where these features of the Internet and characteristics of online use play out. Sometimes, the features we describe in this chapter pertain to the properties of the technology itself, i.e., to platforms, services, applications, algorithms, data, and software. Sometimes they pertain to features of the human psychology of users. Often, however, the characteristics we describe refer to the interplay between features of human psychology and features of the technology.

Some characteristics of this interplay are becoming increasingly "loud and clear," such as, for example, where use of the technology is recognized as "designed for addiction," or to be "especially" persuasive in ways that are morally troubling. We discuss some problems of online addiction ahead, where features of the technology, and how to use it, exploit some of our vulnerabilities. It is plain, however, that quite generally, across whether our activities are good, bad, or innocuous, that various features of the technology, and of how to use it, are designed to get us "hooked" – and in very mundane, everyday ways. It is, for example, difficult to resist a so-called "listacle" with ten things that characterize "real leaders," or a video with five of the scariest moments ever in the history of aviation, or a new photo a friend has

---

[4] *Ibid.*

posted online, or the feature of "endless scrolling." Features of the interplay between the design of online worlds and human psychology, must, of course, be a focus of any discussion regarding the moral status of our online worlds, and what, if anything, might make them especially morally problematic. Our more specific aims in this regard are to illustrate how characteristics of our online environments produce forms of moral fog that obscure the relevance of our moral sensibilities, to provide an analysis of this obfuscation, and to show how it enables evildoing.

At this point, it is important to note, that there is a bigger, background picture against which these characteristics of our online lifeworlds (and discussions of their impact) must be placed. First, there is the rise of the new platform economies of the Internet, in which companies such as Facebook, Airbnb, Uber, Amazon, eBay, and Alibaba play an important role. These platform economies (where a platform is provided to which users, in particular buyers and sellers, can connect) do not build on traditional asset classes, such as hotels, cars, and consumer goods. Data and information are their key assets, and they exploit features of "multisided markets" that coordinate the behavior of many different types of buyers and sellers – often with deleterious consequences for those working with traditional business models. Think, for example, what Amazon has meant to your local bookstore, Uber to the local taxi drivers, and Airbnb for the small hotels down town.

Internet platforms, in general, have made excellent use of "network" effects. With every new member of, say, LinkedIn or Facebook, the network becomes more valuable. A telephone network, for example, which allows you to call only two people, is obviously far less valuable than one that allows you to call 200 people, even if the former may be better in some other ways, such as being much cheaper. The more people on Facebook, the more value accrues to it, the less attractive it becomes to exit, and the more likely it becomes that you are willing to pay the price associated with subscribing to it. Payment could take the form of cash, time invested, or user data or metadata provided – usually a combination. The end result is that you get locked in.

This has happened for a good number of services that Google offers, and the same holds true for Facebook. Since, for example, children cannot afford not be online, not to be on Facebook, WhatsApp, and Snapchat, and academics need to have a LinkedIn account, or a Google scholar account, these platforms grow. It has already become very difficult to see how we could return to a world without Facebook and Google search engines.

The second part of the bigger picture is the fact that there is constant exchange and interaction between: (a) big data, such as the extremely large volumes of user data and metadata collected by (notably) Google, Facebook, Twitter, and WhatsApp; (b) advanced Artificial Intelligence, machine-learning and data analytics to analyze and classify user behavior online, and; (c) advanced behavioral science, psychometrics, and choice modelling. The elements of this triad are rapidly and constantly augmenting each other. As a result, they enormously increase capabilities and knowledge about how the online world works, what makes people tick, how they feel, how they can be nudged, and how their decisions can be influenced – through buying, voting, watching and clicking. And all of this is in the hands of commercial parties. The intelligence to mine and analyze the data is constantly used to tweak and improve services and products with an eye to their profitability, addictiveness, and nudging potential. All users are constantly subject to large behavioral experiments (without their realizing). Slight differences in choice architectures and website design are presented to find out which will give rise to the most desired outcomes, in terms of sales, time spent on a site, and click-through rates.

The wide-ranging and deep insights into the social world, and the preferences, sentiments, and behavior of individual users, can be sold to the highest bidder, whoever that is. This raises some serious questions about who is responsible for the quality of life, the nature of democracy, the psychological wellbeing of citizens, and for the wide range of phenomena of evil online we see unfold every day. These are the sort of questions we are now quite used to discussing in other domains, notably more familiar "tragedy of the commons" type cases, such as the problem of climate change. There, for example, we ask: what are the responsibilities of the fossil fuel industry in light of climate change and the environmental problems the world is facing? What are the responsibilities of the individual car driver, the bus company owner, the car manufacturer? What about the government, the environmental protection agency, the climate and energy scientists, or Greenpeace? So too, we should now be discussing such questions a great deal more about our online worlds, and with far more attention to deeper worries about the fate of the prosocial, moral life, as we increasingly live online.

Churchill's famous remark about the impact of our built environment also applies to the architecture of our digital environments. Our online "buildings" are primarily shaped by the big Five IT companies – Google, Facebook, Amazon, Microsoft, and Apple. There is hardly any moral or political reflection on the types of societies shaped by the digital technology that constitutes our new "online lifeworld." So we need to start identifying issues, and developing our thoughts a good deal more, especially concerning the nature of our basic values, and the impact of features of our environments upon them. Moreover, any thoughts we do develop will need to be inscribed into our new digital technology. Otherwise, since we will almost certainly not be going back to some pre-Internet world, our understandings about the prosocial life and how to support it will have no effect at all. We need to think about justice, fairness, equality, human rights, human dignity, and so on, in terms of software, algorithms, computer data, and Internet cables and platforms, lest our thoughts become irrelevant and obsolete. And since it is commercial parties, in particular our big five companies, that have so much of the power and control, this probably means we cannot leave it up to them, and the IT industry, to lead the charge in identifying, and developing ways to address, the social and moral problems their products and services are implicated in bringing about.

Many of the features of our online environment that we discuss below are "Janus faced." They help us to better understand the worrying phenomena we present in this book, but at the same time they also help explain the great success and attractiveness of online environments.

We start with three fundamental features of this sort – epistemic success, connectivity, and coordination.

2.2 Epistemic Success, Connectivity, and Coordination

2.2.1 Epistemic Success

The Internet is an extraordinarily valuable tool for gaining knowledge. A spectacularly rich learning environment with online databases, journals, encyclopedias, open source publications, wikis, blogs, and news feeds. As a way of acquiring knowledge, use of the Internet differs significantly from traditional practices, such as going to the library, taking out books, reading them and returning them, or subscribing to a newspaper, and perhaps taking out the clippings and keeping them in a shoe box to search through later. These different ways of getting knowledge (or epistemic practices) can be compared and evaluated on the basis of a number of characteristics. Two main ones are reliability and fecundity.[5]

The reliability of a practice for gaining knowledge can be spelt out in terms of the ratio of true beliefs one acquires, compared to false and other beliefs one acquires, by engaging in the practice. So, for instance, your average lunch conversation with colleagues at a non-financial institution is likely to leave you with a fairly low ratio of true beliefs about the global financial crisis, compared to what you would get by studying a *Financial Times* background article on the GFC. Some queries have certainly been raised about the reliability of the Internet as an epistemic practice. Recently, for example, due to the problem of fake news, many have become worried about the reliability of gaining knowledge online about "real" news. As a result, however, Facebook and online media have started to think about ways to filter, monitor, and fact-check. And while Wikipedia, and many open source databases modelled after the Wiki principle, certainly faced

[5] Here we follow Alvin Goldman. For his much fuller account, see, Alvin I. Goldman, *Epistemology and Cognition*, Cambridge, MA: Harvard University Press, 1986.

much initial skepticism, they have become fairly reliable sources of information. Also, many systems of certifying the quality of information have been introduced (especially in specific domains, such as health care information).

The Internet has moved well beyond its initial stage where it was a garbage can of "information." It is no longer an environment where, so far as getting correct answers to questions goes, it could be quite difficult to tell true from false. In fact, it has plainly become (generally) a very reliable tool for acquiring knowledge across a staggering range of fronts. As such, it is an environment of incredible epistemic power, defined in terms of its capacity to help people get true answers to questions (just about any questions) that they might have.

Second, the online environment is fecund. Fecundity refers to the number of people to which true or false ideas may spread in a given unit of time, by means of a knowledge practice. Today there is almost no better way to spread your message to the largest possible audience than through the web. The Internet is also a wonderfully low-cost and efficient medium for getting true beliefs about a given subject. It allows one access to a wealth of information and communication at very low cost. Arguably, when these criteria are used, the Internet is a remarkably successful knowledge environment. You can find useful and true information relevant to your question or problem very easily and quickly, at almost zero cost, and you are likewise enabled to share this information with innumerable others.

2.2.2 Connectivity

The Internet connects people and makes communication, interaction, and transactions between them easy and cheap. It has become the epitome of connections between people. We now live in a "hyperconnected" world which has brought communication, interactions and transaction between individuals to a whole new level. In 1967 Stanley Milgram conducted research that demonstrated that we live in a "small world."[6] A world, as commonly known now, where we are

[6] Stanley Milgram, "The Small World Problem," *Psychology Today*, 1, no. 1, May 1967, pp. 61–67.

only "six degrees of separation" from one another. This "small world" phenomenon has now also been studied in the Facebook environment. To mark its 12th birthday Facebook set out to test this "six degrees of separation" theory. It turned out that if you randomly pick two of Facebook's almost 2 billion users, the "degree of separation" between them is, on average, 3.57 instead of the 6 of our traditional worlds. The degree of connectivity is almost twice as high in the online world.[7]

Notwithstanding these remarkable features of social networks, the social fabric – contrary to what Facebook and social media entrepreneurs want us to believe – stands in stark contrast to the one constituted by the face-to-face interaction, and intimate knowledge and emotional ties that have characterized human communities for many thousands of years. In traditional worlds people lived in smaller communities, with a small number of very close friends, family and others with whom they had "strong ties." Now we have a world of artificial communities, with a large number of superficial and weak ties to a vast number of people through social network platforms such as, Facebook, Twitter, Instagram, and Snapchat. This is just one of the problematic features of our living online that is so rapidly and fundamentally transforming the nature of social life, and that we investigate in the next chapter.

2.2.3 *Coordination*

The Internet is a formidable way to support coordination and collaboration, and so to support the joint and collective pursuit of common goals. One notable example of effective and efficient coordination enabled online is presented by the two-sided markets of the Internet platform economies we mentioned above. Two-sided markets and platforms, like Uber, Airbnb and eBay, allow buyers and sellers, demand and supply, to find each other, and to coordinate their behavior and engage in interactions, transactions, and collaboration. If you are

[7] For discussion of the test, see, for example, http://www.telegraph.co.uk/technology/2016/02/04/facebook-says-there-are-actually-357-degrees-of-separation/ (accessed 13 November 2017).

looking for something very special, or just about anything, you will almost certainly find it on eBay. In its first four years eBay grew to 5 million users. It has been the fastest-growing business in the world. Similarly, the online environment has enabled the coordination of flashmobs, protests and petitions as never before – with enormous reach, at low cost, and organized very quickly.

In China the capacity for coordination of the medium is often exploited to organize buyers and consumers, and get them together to obtain quantum discounts in shops. In no time it is possible to get together a group of people who are interested in buying, say, a certain type of washing machine. If they are united, they can exploit their bargaining position with the manufacturer or shop to get a discount. In citizen science projects, and Amazon Mechanical Turk,[8] many can work together to solve problems and produce answers to questions. Just as criminals and terrorists also use the medium for disseminating and acquiring knowledge, for being connected to others, for planning and coordinating actions, and to enable them to pursue their criminal or terrorist aims in unprecedented ways. The preparation, planning and execution, for instance, of both the bombing of the Spanish train system in 2004, and the 9/11 attack on the World Trade Center in New York in 2001, relied upon these features of the Internet.

Likewise, people who would have considered themselves the only one with a strange idea or sexual preference in the days before the Internet now go online to find fellow-travelers. When a man in Germany decided to find someone who wanted to be killed and eaten by him, it took only a little while to identify someone, get in touch online, and stage a morbid sexual encounter. We know the details of the case because the perpetrator, Armin Meiwes, videotaped the whole procedure, and was convicted for killing his victim after having eaten his private parts and storing the rest of the body in deep freeze for later consumption.[9] Without the Internet and the dark corners of

[8] Amazon Mechanical Turk is an Internet marketplace that connects individuals and businesses to find, assemble and coordinate human intelligence to undertake tasks that computers cannot carry out.

[9] For discussion of the case, see, for example, https://www.theguardian.com/world/2003/dec/04/germany.lukeharding (accessed 15 November 2017).

the deep web hidden from plain site, it would have been impossible, or at least extremely difficult, to find like-minded people and make these fantasies come true. The same applies to the grooming and child pornography cases we described in Chapter 1.

In addition to these features – epistemic success, connectivity, and coordination – a number of other features of our online environments shed light on how evil online gets traction. Indeed, as we have suggested, without a deeper understanding of such features, and hence of the ways in which people are guided by, and related to one another by, Internet applications, it would often be difficult to understand people's online behavior. We begin, for instance, by describing how online recommender systems and algorithms support a selectivity that creates so-called "echo chambers" and "filter bubbles."[10] These features of online environmental design help create a narrow-mindedness about the way that the world is experienced. Without an appreciation of the impact of such features, the phenomenon of narrow-mindedness online becomes very difficult to understand. Given the unique exposure the Internet offers to just about everything, and so the unique opportunity it offers to *expand* one's horizons, you might reasonably expect that a broadening and opening of minds would be the more dominant result.

2.3 Other Features of Online Worlds that Shape Our Lives

2.3.1 Selectivity

Infrastructures, software, and applications present affordances but also constraints. The algorithms that social media run determine, for instance, which new items and posts from friends you get to see, how you are able to present yourself to others, and how far your reach into the social world extends. The online world has many applications, and a rapidly increasing number of them are geared towards individual search profiles and user histories, and preferences as they are revealed in clicks, streams, configurations, purchases from App stores, and online behavior.

[10] See, Eli Pariser, *The Filter Bubble: What the Internet is Hiding From You*, London: Penguin Press, 2011.

Cass Sunstein has highlighted the phenomenon of "the daily me" to describe the adaptation of the flow of information in online worlds to a profile of individual users and their preferences.[11] Newspapers and news sites use profiling techniques to customize the provision of information to readers on the basis of the preferences they reveal in their online activity. Learning algorithms that work on the collected data of individual users of websites are used to create profiles of users, which are then deployed to provide users with further content that is similar or related (and so likely to be appreciated). If, for instance, you are an aficionado of freestyle wrestling, a watcher of prankster videos, interested in Italian cuisine, or a fan of Chopin, and you use YouTube to access your favorite subjects, you will be fed with more of the same. On the basis of your search history, online content platforms build a profile and customize it further to develop a "filter bubble" – your own little world, or "bubble," where most other things are filtered out. Your current and future experience and activity is thereby narrowed down, tending to be increasingly limited to content similar to the attitudes and interests your search history has revealed.

If your "daily me" has been built by selecting sports instead of international politics, you will not hear much about developments in foreign affairs; if you indicate that you are interested in rowing, you won't be presented with information about soccer; and so on. As a result, between you and the technology, you develop narrow-mindedness. As Sunstein observes, this puts an axe to the very idea of the broadly informed citizen, and damages the notion of parliamentary democracy that is built upon this idea.[12]

Another design feature of our online environments that seems to fragment society was identified by David R. Johnson and David Post in the early days of the Internet. They pointed out that the costs of leaving an online community, group, or game, and joining another,

---

[11] Cass Sunstein, *Republic.com*, Princeton, NJ, Princeton University Press, 2002. As Sunstein notes, he did not coin the term "the daily me." It was coined by Nicholas Negroponte, founder of the MIT, Media Lab.

[12] *Ibid.*

were, in principle (as a consequence of the design of the Internet), much lower than exiting, and/or joining, communities offline. To emigrate, or to go to another city, change school or university, or join another club, involves considerable switching costs. Johnson and Post predicted, on the basis of the fact that switching costs are close to zero online, that a rapid "speciation" of normative communities will occur. Instead of engaging with, much less adjusting to, the normative regime of groups to which we belong, we will simply swap our normative environment.[13]

Such opportunities, of course, can be a very good thing – most obviously where our normative regime is something we really should escape. However, our new-found mobility also makes it fatally easy to avoid thinking about our preferences, attitudes, and conduct. In particular, it enables us to avoid self-examination in light of the different and revisionary views presented by others, and by the conventions, rules, and laws that make up the community of which we are currently members. It becomes increasingly easier to screen out exposure to varied and alternative interests, attitudes, ideas, and ways of life that might take us beyond our current selves. And it becomes increasingly easier to screen out any feedback in the form of critical, reflective dialogue about our current selves.

In our traditional worlds, most of us cannot (so easily) confine our experiences, and the life we share with others, to those that address and reinforce our pre-existing attitudes and preferences. It is difficult to avoid exposure to a raft of different directions and revisions that others put to us. Moreover, this is a very good thing – as, for instance, not only illustrated by ideals of deliberative democracies, but also commonly instantiated in both our personal relationships and our working lives. In the next chapter, we develop a broader picture of the morally significant contrasts between our online and traditional social worlds, and a larger story about the broad range of basic values that are at stake now that we live online so much.

---

[13] David R. Johnson and David Post, "Law and Borders: The Rise of Law in CyberSpace," *First Monday*, Vol. 1 No. 1. 1996. http://firstmonday.org/article/view/468/389 (accessed 17 November 2017).

2.3.2 Homophily and Stigmergy[14]

An often-remarked phenomenon that can drive online conduct and also bring problems of unthinking, narrow-mindedness, is "Homophily" – the tendency of individuals to associate and bond with similar others, as in the proverb "birds of a feather flock together."[15] Homophily has been discovered in many network studies. Similarity (notably in age, gender, class, and organizational role) breeds connection, and social networking websites like Facebook foster homophilic atmospheres. When a Facebook user likes or interacts with an article or post of a certain kind, Facebook will follow up by showing the user further similar posts (as noted above regarding creating user profiles and customizing content). This fosters homophily, which, in turn, adds to the size and effectiveness of "echo chambers" on social networking sites, so that only people of similar interests, attitudes and ideologies interact with each other (hence "echo" one another). A familiar, problematic version of this phenomenon is "copycat" behavior. Copycat problems are very prominent online, and are high on the watch list of law enforcement and mental health professionals alike. Some types of crime and suicide are very easily copied – as the rise of so-called suicide pacts online attests. "Happy slapping" and some of the other cases from Chapter 1 also illustrate the problem.

The phenomenon of "stigmergy" has also been identified as a driver of online conduct in this context. Stigmergy was first described in studies of animal behavior, observed in the behavior of ants and termites who mark trails. Every individual that takes the trail marks its path with pheromones which slightly increase the likelihood that others will take the same path. Online likes and visitor numbers can have the same effect as pheromone trails. A large number of likes, and large numbers of followers and visitors, signify great interest, and in so doing significantly increase interest that will be shown by "passers-by." "Likes, follows, and visits"

---

[14] For definitions see the Wikipedia entries https://en.wikipedia.org/wiki/Homophily and https://en.wikipedia.org/wiki/Stigmergy.

[15] See, Miller McPherson, Lynn Smith-Lovin, and James M. Cook, "Birds of a Feather: Homophily in Social Networks," *Annual Review of Sociology*, 27, 2001, pp. 415–444.

are typically a prominent feature of online settings, both across our more public and private lives – across, for example, how we present ourselves on Facebook, on our websites, on eBay, or how we might present our businesses. And as we saw in Chapter 1, across cases as diverse as pranks online and radicalization to terror online, following increasingly popular trails can obscure conflicting moral sensibilities, and, as a trail gains something of a life of its own, lead people wildly astray.

2.3.3 *Jurisdiction*

The Internet as such is not under the jurisdiction of one or more nation-states. It is, therefore, often not clear which laws apply, apart from the local laws which may apply to users or intermediaries who are based in a particular country, such as ISPs or telecom providers and cable companies, or content producers. Users who physically reside in a country fall under that country's law, and companies may fall under that law too. If any country has control over the Internet as such, it would be the United States, since it has control over the root of the system, the domain-name server. The US-based ICANN (Internet Corporation for Assigned Names and Numbers) is the organization responsible for the assigning of names and thinking about so-called top-level domain names (.gov,.edu,.org, and so on). Though ICANN has some multilateral representation, the servers on which the roots are kept are in the United States. Multiple discussions, debates, political quarrels, and legal procedures continually occur regarding disputes and conflicts of interest happening in cyberspace, most often eventually transferred to a jurisdiction in the offline world. In the meantime, however, financial information, ransomware, cyberattacks, and terrorist videos travel across the Internet and reach their targets, without the enforcement agencies of the victims' countries being able to attribute the crimes effectively and take action. All this gives Internet users the impression that cyberspace and the online world is a globalized, rapidly changing realm, without clear rules, and without dedicated enforcement and governance.

2.3.4 Anonymity

The Internet requires unique identification of devices and the system of unique addresses for websites (URLs), part of the basic design of the Internet, is designed to ensure accurate delivery of packets of information. Along with devices that are uniquely identified and identifiable, the cameras of these devices, the behavioral patterns associated with sessions, and biometric identification[16] will uniquely identify users. Nevertheless, there is a great deal of anonymity and obfuscation of identities online, and we often do not know who is behind the keyboard.

Indeed, since the arrival of artificial intelligence, it is not always clear that one is dealing with a human being rather than an artificial agent. In the 1960s, Joseph Weizenbaum showed how easily people can be deceived. He programmed a software program, ELIZA, that would take on the role of a psychiatrist, answering and posing questions. Many people who interacted remotely with ELIZA thought they were chatting with a human being. Today, it is sometimes hard to find out whether we are talking and interacting with a bot – a computer program that can, as Weizenbaum's experiment illustrated, be relatively simple. Certainly, it can be very difficult to make out whether someone is telling the truth, or overselling themselves.[17]

Cases concerned with elaborate deception about identity online, such as catfishing, exploit this feature, as, typically, does grooming, and, often, cyberbullying. Further, one can interact with others by means of anonymizers – services which technically obscure one's identity, or assign a pseudonymous identity. However, since the Internet retains a lot of information about one's online use, expert users, such as hackers, or agents of intelligence or secret service organizations, may nevertheless find out a great deal about would-be deceivers if they need to.

---

[16] Biometric identification in computer science refers to the identification of individual users through human characteristics that individuate people, such as fingerprints, face recognition, iris and retina scans, and signatures.

[17] For his account of his experiment undertaken at MIT in the 1960s, see Joseph Weizenbaum, *Computer Power and Human Reason: From Judgment to Calculation*, San Francisco: W. H. Freeman and Company, 1976.

2.3.5 *Virtuality*

A girl walks with her mother on the beach and finds a jellyfish. She looks carefully at it, pokes it with a stick and exclaims "look mummy how realistic." Confusing a representation with the real thing is a familiar feature of our traditional worlds. In virtual worlds our sense-data are caused by the virtual reality gear, software, and simulations we use. In many ways, virtual worlds are not real worlds. A virtual reality rainstorm, for instance, does not leave us all wet, nor does a virtual car bring us home from work. On the other hand, we can feel scared or dizzy, be moved to tears, pursue interests, and have our normative outlook shaped by our virtual worlds. So even if they are not real in some ways, or are not fully realistic in some ways, our virtual worlds can certainly be real (or real enough) in terms of their cognitive and affective impact. And while we are getting used to increasingly inhabiting artificial and virtual worlds, sorting out what is real and virtual remains problematic and confusing.

Many applications on the World Wide Web and Internet are referred to as virtual worlds. There is very realistic virtual child pornography: children are not used, the effects are produced by very realistic animations derived from visualization techniques. There are also virtual homicides and virtual rapes. The computer games and worlds that are used for gaming are becoming more realistic with advances in their resolution, rendering, and dynamics. Often animations are based on scientific models of certain parts of the real world, for instance, using human models to render wrinkling of skin and muscle tissue, refraction of light on skin, and so on. Unsurprisingly, therefore, for users who are immersed in such virtual worlds, the boundaries between what is real and not real can become confused and unclear – as, for instance, the defense "it was just a posting on a website" often reveals in cases of online bullying and shaming.

2.3.6 *Voluntariness*

The channel, modalities and granularity, time, place, and context of being online can be largely self-chosen. As many of us now recognize, social media accommodate self-aggrandizement. "Rich kids on Instagram" are the summit to which many now aspire online.

Certainly, on social media hardly anyone is dull or boring. Holidays always look splendid. Everyone is happy all the time. Failures and disappointments have no place. The possibilities for customizing how one comes across are virtually endless. Dating is now also an App affair, undertaken through Tinder or similar websites, allowing one to swipe people into the interesting versus uninteresting batch instantly. Our self-presentations and engagement with one another in these highly voluntary kinds of ways, including (increasingly) across our personal and intimate lives, has been given enormous impetus by the design of our online-transformed worlds.

Everyone online, and in our traditional worlds, has to engage in a certain amount of self-presentation of the more, seemingly, "voluntary" kind, i.e. one consciously chooses how to present oneself for particular purposes, and/or in particular contexts, such as in working life. However, people are now increasingly judged on the basis of what searches on Google return on them. Recruiters and human resources staff, for example, often report that the Google search says it all, or, at the least, provides important context to the application letter or the job interview. Google knows how to crosslink search data and IP addresses with search terms and search profiles. You can keep track of yourself and others, and so, for example, find out who is more prominent on the web, you or your colleague. Most of us are now aware of the enormous reputational importance that can attach to how we look online, and so we have strong reason to be concerned about how we present ourselves online.

Accordingly, people tend to spend a lot of time constructing their websites and their social media pages. Some of them are real artworks. Again, however, the normative impact of worlds where people's understanding of themselves, and of their relations with others, is dominated by highly voluntary forms of self-presentation is mixed. In our next chapter we argue that there are significant broad-based worries for the self, and for social relationships with others, that come with this trend.

2.3.7 Positionality

Economists define goods as having positionality when the goods' value depends on how they are distributed among a population, rather than on how many there are in total. My knowledge, for example, about a forthcoming merger of companies has a particular value to me, on the condition that you don't know about it. Positional goods impart status: if you have a big car, mine needs to be bigger. If the peacock's tail is long, the rival's tail needs to be longer. The phenomenon is also present in high-frequency trading. Large volumes of shares are often automatically traded in very short periods of time, often just seconds or split seconds. Information is of the essence, and if I know something just a nanosecond before you do, the profit will be mine and not yours.[18]

The online world is a locus of positionality. It easily generates and nourishes arms races, for attention, money, advertisements, air time, eyeballs, banners, holiday photographs on Facebook, and embellished resumés. All because comparison is so easy and unavoidable, and is greatly enhanced by the platform economies of the Internet, whether users are connected to the platform as buyers and sellers, or as individuals engaging in self-expression or seeking social connection. In terms of outrageous content, as we saw in the case of some prankster videos, positionality is the mechanism largely responsible for giving the trend traction. We discuss in some more detail how positionality can send us astray in section 4.3.3.

2.3.8 Interpretive Flexibility

Interpretive flexibility was first introduced in the context of social studies of science and technology[19]. A paradigm case is the development of the bicycle. At an early stage of development, there were two rival conceptions of the bicycle. There was the unwieldy "Ordinary" or penny-farthing, with one big wheel and one very small wheel, and there was the immediate precursor of our present bicycle. There were not only two different designs, but also two very different ideas attached to each. The big unwieldy bicycle was mostly used by young men dressed in sports clothing, who wanted to show off. It required a lot of stamina and skill to ride the thing; it was by no means

[18] More on some of the normative implications of this in Chapter 4. See also Robert H. Frank, The Darwin Economy: Liberty, Competition and the Common Good, Princeton University Press, U.S., 2011.

[19] See, Wiebe E. Bijker, Thomas P. Hughes and Trevor Pinch (eds), The Social Construction of Technological Systems: New Directions in the Sociology and History of Technology, Cambridge, Mass. MIT Press, 2012.

a vehicle of convenience. The other design was more practical, since it was an easy and relatively cheap way to get from A to B quite quickly. As we know, the latter conception became the dominant bicycle design. The flexibility in the development of the bicycle refers to the short period over 100 years ago when another way of looking at the idea of the bicycle could have become the dominant frame – before closure was reached in favor of the present bicycle.

Interpretive flexibility, hence, refers to the degrees of freedom in the interpretation and the assignment of meaning to new technologies and artifacts. Only when the ambiguity of different interpretations by different social groups and rivalling descriptions disappears can certain robust meanings be assigned to new devices and technologies, and the moral connotations and implications become clearer. New, dynamic, and complex technology establishes an especially uncertain environment with respect to the application of our conventional understandings, including our moral understandings. The online revolution has become a spectacular example of this – getting our heads around the new phenomena was and remains difficult, there persists a lack of clarity about how to interpret our new worlds and how to describe our own attitudes and actions within them.

2.3.9 Interactivity

One of the standard observations – which is nevertheless true – that is often made when new media are compared to old media, such as television, is that the new media, and the Internet in particular, are interactive. New media allow both synchronous and asynchronous interaction between sender and receiver of information. So the users in an online environment are often active in a sense that television-watchers are not, although television-watchers may also, of course, be passively affected or aroused by what they see, and learn from what they consume. Internet users are always ready to be called into communicative action, by responding, entering into a conversation, uploading information, making changes to a site, joining a game, or clicking through a link. This potential for action brings with it a different kind of mental state in the consumer concerning how they are engaged with, and relate to, others and the world.

After watching a television program while sitting on a couch, the external world has not changed as a result of the one-way information consumption. However, after a one hour session on the Internet, the world has been changed as a result of the actions of the user. Information has been added, e-mails have been written, cookies have been triggered, log files have been generated, and files have been downloaded. Unlike the consumption of television, the interactivity of the Internet works against passive consumption of content and engages people in ways where they can affect others and the world around them. Again, while in many ways this is a great good, it can just as well be a disaster, such as we see in cases like encouraging others to anorexia or suicide, or where large groups are enlisted to shame or bully people.

2.3.10 Publicity

The Internet has a special attraction: individuals and groups can very easily and broadly express themselves and communicate to the world. As a result, an avalanche of valuable material, but also of both relatively innocuous and shocking material has been triggered. The special attraction, for example, of beating up a stranger in the street and live streaming it is only that it can be posted online. Had it not been for the Internet this would not have happened. And while, for example, decapitations are nothing new, the Internet has provided the means to publicize such terror in a way that we have never seen before, and has been exploited accordingly.

The online revolution has also raised significant issues about how we are to understand the status of the online world in terms of the traditional distinction between the public and private realms. The distinction is highly relevant, for example, if you want to establish whether someone is guilty of defamation, slander or has given offense, by remarks on websites and Internet forums, social network sites, and weblogs. Are these contexts essentially private or public? Is spreading rumors or insulting people online to be compared to yelling abusive language in the street, or to the loose banter one shares with friends or family in private settings, or to publishing the rumors or insults in a daily newspaper?

One obvious and common reply is to say that where one expresses "private" comments, photos and so on in the public realm, such as a blog or tweet to the world, then one is liable for the reactions and responsibilities that doing so brings. However, online worlds have provided a platform for our private lives in a way that no other medium ever has. Expressing our private selves publicly online has caught on like wildfire and is massive core online business. A major effect of this rapid collapsing of the public/ private contrast has been the confusion of boundaries. Indeed, there have been many cases where even those well-experienced in media presentations and navigating the public realm have come undone.

For the rest of us, the general public, inexperienced in navigating mass publicity, boundary confusions about our public/ private lives flourish online. Of particular concern is the vulnerability of our young people to such delusions, and their practice of posting personal details and private information on social networking sites. Again, the usual response is to urge young people to understand that their personal information displayed online is not private but often widely publicized. And even where you think, and sometimes have good reason to think, your personal information is securely private, in one way or another it can often turn out otherwise. (Sexting and revenge porn are commonplace examples.) While this is plainly good advice so far as it goes, features of the Internet and of how it is used work against seeing things so clearly. There is, for instance, the problem of "everyone else is doing it" and the social pressure to position oneself relative to others that goes with it. So while I might be told of the public, rather than private, nature of much Internet interaction, and of the dangers that go with this, I might not see the force of these claims very clearly, if, for example, I am a teenager and my social standing or social inclusion might depend upon divulging personal details and information online.

There are a myriad of cases where people have made aspects of their private lives public in ways that have victimized others and made victims of themselves. The collapsing of the public and private realms in much online use, however, also raises some more fundamental issues. In particular, it threatens to take with it a raft of our most basic values concerning ourselves and our relations with others. We develop the case for these more fundamental worries in our discussion ahead in Chapter 3.

2.3.11 Domesticity

'Domestication" is a term used in science, technology and media studies to describe the processes by which new technology is appropriated by its users and integrated in to their daily life. Users change their environment and practices in light of new artifacts and devices, and their new modes of living usually feed back into further innovation processes in industry, thereby shaping the next generation of technology. Domestication theory was initially developed to help understand the adoption and use of new media technologies by households. It is now also used to account for technologies and innovations in the workplace, and other social spheres that can be analyzed economically, culturally, and sociologically.

The Internet is now fully domesticated. It is part and parcel of many activities in the household. We introduce the idea of domesticity to refer to the phenomenon of how new and often surprising, worrisome, and alien information and images can enter into one's familiar and private environment. This means, among other things, that Internet content is viewed and generated in familiar settings and combined and integrated with other homely activities, such as eating, relaxing, or watching television. Thus, evil content, just as well as good and innocuous content, has become entrenched in our everyday lives and become associated with the most ordinary and normal of activities, such as having breakfast, getting dressed and listening to music. People may be munching their cereals while watching video footage of terrorist decapitations. The Internet has given significant new meanings, of both degree and kind, to domesticity. One of the consequences being that we fail to appreciate the truly horrible or appalling nature of the events and actions we are exposed to online, because we consume them as part of our familiar lives, in our everyday, private settings.[20]

---

[20] See also, our discussion ahead in Chapter 4 on the shared life and our vulnerability to evil.

2.3.12 Isolation

As the story of the *Batavia* illustrates, it is also clear that in many cases of evil *offline*, such factors as (believed) moral isolation and risk reduction have played a significant role in the flourishing of evil. The relevance of forms of isolation online has also been well documented in certain cases. In the early years of life online, for example, the phenomenon of apotemnophilia, in which individuals desire that their arms or legs be amputated, gained impetus almost exclusively through Internet networks connecting individuals who would support and affirm each other's claim to "define" themselves (usually connected to sexual image) by amputating their limbs. In his pioneering account of the phenomenon, Carl Elliott noted:

> [M]many wannabes are convinced that amputation is the only possible solution to their problems, yet they have never seen a psychiatrist or a psychologist, have never tried medication, have never read a scientific paper about their problems. More than a few of them have never, ever spoken face to face with another human being about their desires. All they have is the Internet, and their own troubled lives, as the place where those two things intersect.[21]

In Japan not only is there a demographic trend toward an aging population, there is the additional and increasing problem that many of the younger generation do not seem to want to grow up. There is a tendency for young people to stay and live with their parents, because they find it more convenient and can save themselves the money that they like to spend on luxury goods, fashion, and electronic gadgets. A special group of adolescents and young adults living at home with their parents are the *hikikomori*, individuals who have become the victims of the pressures of competitive Japanese society. They prefer to live a highly isolated life, commonly consumed by playing computer videogames in their room.

---

[21] Carl Elliott, "A New Way to be Mad," *The Atlantic Monthly*, December, 2000.

Online worlds have especially enabled such extreme cases of social isolation. In more everyday ways, however, self-expression and engagement with others undertaken in social isolation has become a dominant way of life. There is a lot of interaction between people, chatting, MSN, SNS, e-mailing, and twittering going on, but commonly it is done in physical isolation.

2.3.13 Addictiveness

Recognized in DSM-5, Internet addiction has recently become an official mental disorder. People can become addicted to the idea of being online, checking their Facebook, WhatsApp, and Messenger. It can be quite overwhelming – checking e-mail compulsively both at work and in spare time to the detriment of other tasks. Many studies, such as some we mentioned in Chapter 1, have confirmed this.[22] Another form of addiction is related to the content or nature of the online activities undertaken. Online gambling and pornography are the most prevalent. It is well known from the literature on mental disease that rehearsal, repetition, and addiction to certain behaviors, thoughts, and stimuli are essential to the problem. People have problems with addictive routines, whether they are associated with eating, smoking, sexuality, thrills and adrenaline rushes, gambling, alcohol, or drugs. An example in the design of websites is "click bait" or "endless scrolling" that try to capture and retain attention for as long as possible, and advertise products and services along the way. The research that investigates and develops seduction technology is referred to as "captology," and "persuasive design." It should be clear enough that these built-in values need to be exposed and critically discussed before the products and services in which they are expressed are accepted.

Much evildoing and exposure to evil online, such as many of the cases we described in Chapter 1, have been enabled, either completely, or to some large degree, by the features of online expression and communication presented above. Moreover, many of these features – notably,

[22] See, for instance, Mary Aitken's lengthy discussion of Internet addiction, *op. cit.*

selectivity, anonymity, positionality, domestication, isolation, conflation of public/ private contrasts, high voluntariness, jurisdiction, virtuality, and interpretive flexibility – have enabled the doing and consumption of evil in a particular way. They have created and magnified moral fog in the minds of users.

In our discussions in the following chapters, we develop our account of evildoing, both online and in our traditional worlds, and the varieties of moral fog that enable it. In the next chapter, we develop our account by looking at some general trends in our social words online that undermine some of our basic values. Our primary concern is the conflation and changing contrasts between public and private worlds online. We have already seen how this may play a role in some specific problem cases, such as online shaming and revenge porn. We want to show however, that there are deeper and broader worries for the fate of our prosocial values that come with the demolition of contrasts between the public and the private realms online. We also highlight the driver, well targeted by our online social worlds, of seemingly being able to live life "on one's own terms."

3

The Transformation of Social Life

When I felt annoyed I practiced looking serene, even cheerful; in my enthusiasm I went so far as to suffer pain voluntarily so as to achieve a simultaneous expression of pleasure. I labored with the same care, and even more difficulty, to repress symptoms of unexpected joy. In this way I was able to acquire the power over my features at which I have sometimes seen you so astonished… my thoughts were purely for my own benefit, and I revealed only what I found it useful to reveal.

Dangerous Liaisons[1]

Never trust a man who does not drink.

Humphrey Bogart[2]

3.1 Introduction

The apparent re-drawing of public and private life online has spawned various discussions in academic forums and media stories. Mark Zuckerberg, founder of Facebook, is well known for some bold claims advocating collapsing the private and public realms, and supporting the end of privacy as a social norm (as if privacy were simply a dispensable old-fashioned convention). In some oft-cited quotes he says: "You have one identity… Having two identities for yourself is an

[1] Choderlos De Laclos, *Dangerous Liaisons*, Penguin Classics, pp. 181–182, 2007. (First published by Durand Neveu, France, 1782.)
[2] American actor, 1899–1957.

Evil Online, First Edition. Dean Cocking and Jeroen van den Hoven.

example of a lack of integrity."[3] Many others, have also, in one way or another, argued for the creativity, freedom, and new ways to express or define oneself enabled by the re-drawing of our public and private worlds online.[4]

When people have been worried about how the public and private realms are faring with the online revolution, they have mostly been concerned about the apparent explosion (in degree and kind) in privacy invasion and related harms. Revenge porn is one such current trend. Our concern in this chapter is not with the invasion of privacy and the harms this can bring. Instead we have in mind some broader and deeper worries about the fate of privacy and about the fate of our values generally.[5]

Traditional social worlds enable plural modes of self-expression and communication across both public and private realms. Navigating the many, quite different and sometimes conflicting, considerations thrown up by our inhabiting these two realms imposes, and enables, a range of basic values. We draw attention to: autonomy, privacy, civility, intimacy, and trust. In typical online social worlds, however, many of these values are, or appear to be, expendable. And, as a result, important features of these values are lost, and so is much of the prosocial, moral life they enable.

Most of this chapter aims to add detail to this picture of our online social worlds. In so doing, we also go on to discuss a related problem: the common, though often illusory, driver (well-exploited by our online social worlds), that we seem able to craft our personal/public

---

[3] See David Kirkpatrick, *The Facebook Effect: The Inside Story of the Company that is Connecting the World*, New York: Simon & Schuster, 2010, Chapter 10 "Privacy: You have One Identity," p. 199.

[4] For a thoughtful and hilarious illustration of some of the issues here, see, Mark Maron's TV series, *Maron*, "Professor of Desire," Series 3, Episode 8, 2015.

[5] For another discussion of some broader social worries, see, for example, Helen Nissenbaum, *Privacy in Context: Technology, Policy and the Integrity of Social Life*, Palo Alto, CA: Stanford University Press, 2010.

selves, and so much of our identity and relations with others, largely on our own terms.

3.2 Our Public and Private Lives: Plural Worlds and Values

For most of us, our identity involves a variety of aspects of self. Given the range of interests, relationships, and roles most of us have and the range of contextual circumstances within which these are expressed, an identity without such plurality would be extraordinarily limited and ineffectual: we would be unable to properly pursue various interests and effectively engage in various relationships and roles across a range of contexts. The varied attitudes, desires, personality traits, and so on, across the different contexts of our lives, are also often at some odds with one another. At work, for instance, it may be appropriate that one is industrious, and that one's attention is narrowly directed by the pursuit of specific goals. This would be hopeless – limiting, ineffectual and inappropriate – for relaxing at home with family, or hanging out with friends.[6]

Moreover, plural and conflicting aspects of self are often presented within the context of *one* relationship, role, or encounter. So, for example, we choose to sit with respectful concentration through a boring speech, but we do not choose that our eyes start wandering or our attention flagging, that we become restless, and so forth. We communicate a lot with respect to our thoughts and feelings through tone of voice, facial expression, and body movement, and this can conflict with other self-presentations that we do choose (or would choose). Such conduct, over which we exercise less voluntary choice and control, also often reflects something about us, such as an interest, attitude, feeling, or emotion, and often provides fertile and appropriate grounds for interpretation of oneself, by others, or one's own self-interpretation.

---

[6] And sometimes of course, our pursuit of plural values conflicts, and the price of pursuing one is the cost of another – the pursuit of our family lives, for instance, suffers on account of the time, energy and/or temperament required for the pursuit of our working lives.

So, for instance, I notice my friend's obsession with new shoes, or how she is very "bossy," or her anxiety when we are out together and her ex-partner appears on the arm of his new love. Her obsession with new shoes, her "bossiness," and her anxiety, are not the result of her exercising high levels of choice and control. This is not to say she is altogether out of control. But she certainly did not reflect on these matters and then decide that it would be a good idea to start acting in very bossy ways, or to be obsessed about new shoes, or to be anxious when she bumps into her ex-partner. And she may well have preferred not to have been so anxious, obsessive, or bossy. Nevertheless, the aspects of herself over which she exercises less choice and control present appropriate considerations for me to form impressions that will guide my interaction with her.[7]

So, for instance, because I interpret her as anxious when the ex-partner appears, I try to lighten up the situation with a joke, or some other strategy of distraction. When, for instance, she is forcing her smile with the ex-partner, she is obviously, not as a matter of choice and control, presenting her smile as *forced*. On the contrary, this behavior conflicts with and undermines the self-presentation she aims to make effective – namely, to appear comfortable about seeing the ex-partner on the arm of his new love. Yet, my interpretive interactions are not confined to this self-presentation; if they were so confined she would rightly think me insensitive and failing to act as her friend (or perhaps anyone who ought to recognize the situation and respect her efforts). Accordingly, as her friend, or, say, a work colleague, it may be an expression of intimacy, respect for autonomy, or both, that would move me to engage in the distracting small talk, or to provide cover for her to discreetly exit the room.

Such interpretive interactions are a commonplace of the quite different values of intimacy, civility and autonomy. In ordinary, as well as significant ways, it is upon such interpretive interactions that we commonly express features of intimacy, such as mutual affection and

---

[7] We are not saying here that she is not responsible for these less chosen and controlled aspects of her conduct. If, for instance, she preferred to be less bossy, then her failure to do something about it might be her fault. We discuss the issue of attributing responsibility in such cases in Chapter 5.

the disposition to benefit and promote the interests of one another. I express my affection for my friend when I playfully tease her about her bossiness or her obsession with shoes. My lightening up the situation when her ex-partner enters the room exhibits my concern for her welfare. Similarly, it would be disrespectful to the limitations and fragility of my friend's capacities for autonomy to ignore her anxiety and apparent desire to throw a drink in the face of her ex-partner when they unexpectedly meet. The concern then – commonly addressed in terms of respect for individual autonomy and responsibility – to make effective one's reflective choices about how to be, engage with others and live, is not only the proper concern of the individual. Often, also, it is the proper concern of others and is significantly realized as a relational product of one's interpretive interactions with others.

This is the situation in regard my interpretive interactions concerning both the more passive and active self-presentations of my friend (and with those between my friend and her ex-partner). By making small talk and discreetly getting her out of the room in response to her discomfort and anxiety I assist, perhaps crucially, her capacity for autonomy. I (or her ex-partner) would not be respecting her autonomy by making her discomfort and anxiety a public, explicit topic of conversation, or by failing to recognize it, or by ignoring what we see. We do not respect her autonomy by putting aside her more passive self-presentations that threaten to derail how she chooses to present herself. We do not, for instance, take the forced smiles to simply represent smiles. Instead, her capacity to make choices about how to present herself and engage with others, is (partly) made effective, and respected, by our appropriate interpretive reactions in light of the conflicting (more and less chosen and controlled) self-presentations that we see.[8]

The presentation of less chosen aspects of our selves often also provides the object for the expression of certain relational aspects of respect for one another's privacy. For the purpose of respecting the legitimate claim of people to keep some of their thoughts and feelings to themselves, and to have some choice and control over the "self"

[8] Similarly, this story provides a plausible way to fill out what would be recommended by the value of civility in the circumstances.

they present to us for public engagement or scrutiny, we can – and often should – choose not to address what their conflicting, less chosen and controlled, self-presentations might tell us. My friend's ex-partner, for instance, may no longer presume to engage in the private concerns of my friend, and so her anxiety and discomfort at their encounter, while recognized, need not be addressed and subjected to his unwelcome attention. This is one way then, in which relational aspects of our respect for the privacy of others can be shown.

The dissonance between the more and the less active self-presentations provide "tells"[9] in communication and understanding. When, in some highly chosen and controlled way we present ourselves, say, as being comfortable or civil about seeing our ex-partner with his new love, but we do so in the face of quite contrary attitudes, emotions, or feelings, we do not present ourselves as we would in the absence of such conflict. The difference is sourced in two ways. First, our self-directives regarding how we present ourselves have limited scope. For instance, my friend tries valiantly not to twitch and shuffle, but some twitching and shuffling gets through. Second, even putting these less chosen and controlled indicators aside, within the scope of the self-presentations we can affect in more highly chosen and controlled ways, such self-presentations tend not to replicate the self-presentations that they seek to mimic. We do not, for instance, use the same facial muscles when we direct ourselves to smile as we do when we more "naturally" smile, say, because we actually are amused by a good joke.[10]

[9] The noun "tell" has become common parlance. Taken from David Mamet's classic depiction of the con man's art in *House of Games*, Good Times Entertainment, 1987.

[10] Separate neural systems are involved in governing our voluntary and involuntary facial expressions. Thus, for instance, certain stroke victims are able to smile at a joke they find amusing but are unable to direct themselves to smile in the absence of actually being amused. The work of Paul Ekman in cataloguing thousands of facial "micro-expressions" in his Diogenes Project and analyzing their significance is especially substantial and fascinating. For some of Ekman's work, see: Ekman, P. and Friesen, W.V., *Unmasking the Face: A Guide to Recognizing Emotions From Facial Cues*, Upper Saddle River, NJ: Prentice Hall, 1975; Ekman, P. and Rosenberg, E.L., *What the Face Reveals: Basic and Applied Studies of Spontaneous Expression Using the Facial Action Coding System (FACS)*, New York, Oxford University Press, 1997.

Moreover, the difference is often quite noticeable. My friend's smile through gritted teeth when she bumps into the ex-partner and his new love is in stark contrast to the one she was wearing when she last showed me her new pair of shoes. Such "tells," of course, are not necessarily so straightforward. It is not as if the meaning of the dissonance must be plain. Often it is obvious what lies behind, say, the need for an effort to "smile like you mean it." You might, for instance, resent, envy, or simply not much like someone to whom you have to present an award. You might, for instance, have to greet and entertain your teenage daughter's first boyfriend, and be under pressure from your wife to drop the intimidating father persona.

Just as well, however, it is often not so obvious what, say, an awkward smile might be telling us. For instance, I might be the recipient of the aforementioned award. I might know that my presenter does not like me. I might notice his awkward smile. What do I make of it? There are many possibilities depending upon how the story is further described. He might, for example, be envious of me and not want me to be celebrated and this might produce the awkward smile. But he might just as well be trying to get over himself. He might be trying to smile like he means it when in fact he does mean it. Unfortunately, however, he is very self-conscious, especially in my eyes, of himself as having been envious and it is this that drives the need for the effort to smile like he means it. Thus, communication and understanding in this regard may be as open to confusion as it is to clear insight.[11]

Often also, we have good reasons to make the effort to project self-presentations that are at some odds with how we otherwise think or feel. Such self-presentations may be appropriate, polite, kind or even obligatory. Indeed, as many social scientists, psychologists, and philosophers have noted, without the capacity to choose and control self-presentation in the face of internal conflicting forces much joint and social action – where it is necessary that we be able to get along

[11] What is at least minimally clear is that we can use our neural-muscular system to voluntarily suppress and control some various involuntary expressions and responses, but not all, and that in many cases our voluntary expressions differ recognizably from relevantly similar non-voluntary ones. It also seems clear that while some differences provide quite clear "tells," many do not.

with one another, such as in our working lives – would be impossible. Civilized society in general would be impossible. Short of serious and immediate punishments coming our way, we would be jumping the queue at the deli, undermining our colleagues, and doing much worse things whenever we had the impulse to do so. Fortunately, most of us have the relevant capacities in sufficient supply such that we are capable of apprehending, and being guided by, some basic values and reasons, in the face of internal conflicting forces. So, for instance, (while it is hardly foolproof) when the check-out teller at the supermarket asks me how my day has been, while I realize she is not likely to care either way, and I may well have just about had it with this "howdy doody" stuff, I can usually manage not to snap: "What the hell do you care hey!?"

Social scientists have long identified and argued for the necessity and value of psychosocial environments that support this sort of plurality in how we can express ourselves and relate to others. Ervin Goffman's work on the social and contextual frames that govern and direct the information we "give" and the information we "give off" has been especially influential. Goffman pointed to the importance of the acknowledged information for which the person accepts responsibility and the social and relational conventions discouraging focus on the information that is "given off." The self we present for public engagement is pictured as the one over which we can exercise sufficient choice and control[12] in presenting to others and so the one over which we can claim (sufficient) responsibility.

More recently, Thomas Nagel has also drawn attention to how conventions of privacy, concealment, non-acknowledgement, or of "putting aside" various aspects of one another serve to provide a psychosocial environment that supports individual autonomy and enables civilized engagement with others.[13] Nagel points out that social conventions of concealment are not just about secrecy and deception, but also reticence and non-acknowledgement. And the latter enable us to

[12] Ervin Goffman, *The Presentation of Self in Everyday Life*, New York: Doubleday Anchor, 1959.

[13] Thomas Nagel, "Concealment and Exposure," *Philosophy and Public Affairs*, 27, no. 1 Winter 1998, p. 4.

present ourselves for appropriate and fruitful interactions in our roles and relations with others, without being overwhelmed by the influence of others or self-consciousness of the awareness of others – in particular, regarding distracting or conflicting aspects of ourselves over which we do not exercise the same sort of choice and control in presenting.

We are thus not condemned or simply in receipt of unwelcome attention for aspects of ourselves we do not actively present for public engagement, and we have a valuable space within which to engage in our own imaginary and reflective worlds – enabling, for instance, relaxation, enjoyment, self-development, and understanding. By supporting our capacity for choice and control over the self that we present for engagement in our relations and roles with others such social and relational conventions of privacy support individual autonomy and responsibility.

However, as we have seen, the value of our interpretive interactions regarding plural and often un-cooperative self-presentations, is not limited to, and would often be mischaracterized by, a singular focus on non-acknowledgement and the respect for autonomy, responsibility and privacy shown by "putting aside" aspects of self not chosen for public engagement. Instead, we commonly respect one another's autonomy, not by simply "putting aside" less chosen, and conflicting, aspects of one another, but by recognizing and responding well to such conflicts. And we commonly (and quite rightly) expect this of one another. The influence of others upon our capacities for autonomy, responsibility, and privacy is not just a hindrance, or unwelcome interference, from which we need some asylum. The influence of others also, importantly, enables our capacities to achieve such values.

As noted above, the value of privacy, for instance, is often both a condition for and realized as a relational product of one's interpretive interactions with others. Both my friend and her ex-partner may rightly regard their discomfort and anxiety at their chance meeting to be a concern which each may no longer presume to address "out loud." Nevertheless, they cannot, or cannot very successfully, keep what they rightly regard private from one another's view. However, they can realize respect for one another's privacy, not simply by setting aside, say, the discomfort and anxiety they may see, but through appropriate interpretive interactions in light of the discomfort and anxiety they do see. Thus, for example, they may keep eye contact fleeting, and converse on non-confronting subjects before wrapping things up quickly. And, again, this is what we may reasonably expect of one another.

Moreover, of course, not only do we not simply confine our interpretive interactions to a person's highly chosen and controlled self-presentations, these self-presentations may also be *in*appropriate, pathetic, or give us the creeps – as, for instance, with many cases of the self-deceived, conceited, or hypocritical. And, while, as Nagel says, conventions of concealment are not just about deception and secrecy, plainly they also have such use. *Dangerous Liaisons* provides some classic, extreme illustrations. Bogart highlights, a little more plainly, how trust can depend upon our having access to the attitudes, desires, and motives of one another's less chosen selves. One kind of such trust concerns whether we can rely on others to fulfill their agreements over time. A good example confirming Bogart's view comes from Robert Frank.[14] He concludes, on the basis of results from experimental game theory, that: "co-operation may be explained less by individual traits of character… than by the nature of the interactions between specific partners."[15] In general, his findings support the claim that the more time people are given to interact and communicate face-to-face, the better they are in predicting who would collaborate with them and who would not.

According to Frank, moral emotions, such as sympathy, facilitate commitment, and their development and refinement were favored during the course of evolution. Indicating commitment through such emotional responses is often crucial for the success of decisions that depend upon the decisions of others. And individuals who have moral emotions and engage face-to-face get more reliable information about how another will behave in specific situations, precisely because of the less chosen and controlled self-presentations of the other to which they do have access.[16]

---

[14] Robert H. Frank, *What Price the Moral High Ground? Ethical Dilemmas in Competitive Environments*, Princeton, NJ: Princeton University Press, 2004.

[15] *Ibid.*, p. 43.

[16] *Ibid.*, pp. 20–21. See also, David Sally, A General Theory of Sympathy, Mind-Reading, and Social Interaction, with an Application to the Prisoners' Dilemma, *Social Science Information*, 39, no. 4, (2000), pp. 567–634.

3.3 Public/Private Lives Online

So how is all of this faring in our social worlds online? We need environments that support the plural realms of public and private social life, since such environments make possible certain kinds of everyday self-expression, interaction, and shared activity that are central features of the prosocial, moral life. So how well do online social worlds support the kind of psychosocial environments we need? We saw in Chapter 1 that quite a lot of recent work undertaken in social psychology is painting a worrying picture. We are now in a position to better see some of the fundamental and varied worries presented by our online social worlds for the prosocial, moral life. For much of the plurality of self-expression, interaction and shared activity across the realms of our public and private worlds, such as expressed by Goffman in terms of what we "give" and "give off," or by Nagel in terms of what we "expose" or "conceal," is lost, or easily marginalized, in our online social worlds.

The design of social communication online especially enables us to go one way (or another) at the expense of the plurality (and the associated values) we have canvassed. Thus, for example, we are especially enabled to make the private public, and so, for instance, we might see a lot more than we would have otherwise, and far more than we would have liked, in relation to my friend's anxiety about bumping into her ex-partner, due to her unloading her feelings online. On the other hand, we are also especially enabled to make the private unavailable altogether. Most likely, for instance, you won't see much about my friend's anxiety at all on her Facebook page. More likely you will see her shopping, partying, and moving onward and upward. In this event, since her anxiety is not available to us, we cannot now violate her right to privacy about it – just as, since it is not available to us, we cannot show respect for her privacy on the matter either. And we cannot support her (efforts at) autonomy and responsibility in trying to deal with it, nor can we form reasons of intimacy in relation to it (more ahead).

We can, of course, express ourselves and interact face-to-face online. Interactive audiovisual worlds, such as provided by Skype, are now common. So perhaps we are not so especially enabled to "give" but not "give off." And, if, for instance, we are already good friends, then what we "give" and "give off" may well be as evident and available for engagement as usual. Nevertheless, as we have seen in our previous chapters, social connection online can help keep at bay much that we might not want to "give off."[17] It remains true, including for any audiovisual interaction we might choose to use, that we are especially enabled to have highly voluntary forms of choice and control over the self we present and express, and over our social interactions and shared activity. Certainly we can avoid much of the shared activity of life that might result, for instance, in bumping into an ex-partner on a night out.

Self-presentation and shared activity in many online social worlds can also enable autonomy and privacy. Had my friend got the news online from her ex-partner about his new love, she could have avoided her conflicting self-presentations altogether, and so been far more convincing about any "well-wishing." So even if they undermine some features of our values, such as some characteristics of autonomy or privacy, online social worlds can also distinctively enable these values in various ways. Indeed, if online communication contexts did allow one to largely suppress unwanted and conflicting self-presentations, and so get them off the playing-field of communication altogether, then one might think privacy and autonomy are better served.[18]

But while there are a variety of such cases, since we want environments that allow or even support the range of prosocial and moral values we have described, blanket suppression would not generally be a good thing. Autonomy and privacy in the virtual case are largely secured at the expense of a pluralism about the self – at the cost, for

---

[17] In addition to the section on self-presentation in Chapter 2, recall also the research from Gardner and Davis described in Chapter 1 highlighting the atypical control over, and concern with, self-presentation, that comes with our online-transformed worlds.

[18] For a discussion of how online social worlds may support some of the values we have discussed, see, for example, Adam Briggle, Real Friends: how the internet can foster friendship, *Ethics and Information Technology*, 10, no. 1, 2008, pp. 71–79.

instance, of losing the relational and social good of respecting the autonomy and privacy of one another that is enabled by our habitation in these plural worlds of public and private life. Similarly, we lose important aspects of the development of intimacy. We may, for example, have a cordial and well-functioning work relationship with another, who we nevertheless see as racked by bitterness and a lack of generosity toward the efforts of his colleagues. He does not "give" us this information. But he "gives it off." So, he may smile and congratulate his colleagues' success *as if* he means it, but we see this associated with conflicting conduct, such as his changing the subject toward his own successes. So long as this sort of thing does not intrude too greatly upon our working relationship, we need not make it our business – much less bring it up with him.

On the other hand, we may make it our business: these considerations may well provide us with reasons for having little interest in pursuing the relationship beyond our working lives together. We may respect his privacy and autonomy by not remarking on his misery and ill-will publicly and explicitly, but our interpretations of his character may well be our reasons for not pursuing a friendship with him. Online, in so far as our self-expression and communication lacks this pluralism, we are less able to create such reasons for, or against, intimacy.

3.4 Life on Your Own Terms

It contributes greatly to a man's moral and intellectual health, to be brought in to habits of companionship with individuals unlike himself, who care little for his pursuits, and whose sphere and abilities he must go out of himself to appreciate.

The Scarlet Letter[19]

The online revolutions in access to information and to one another have provided unprecedented opportunities to expand our knowledge,

[19] Nathaniel Hawthorne, *The Scarlet Letter*, London: Vintage Books, 2008, p. 25. (Originally published Boston: Ticknor and Fields, (1850))

to pursue our social and working lives, and to carry on all sorts of interests and activities. Already, our traditional worlds seem prehistoric in their limitations across these fronts. Transcending these limitations has enabled us to pursue our lives much more on our own terms, unhindered by the barriers to knowledge-acquisition, communication, and the pursuit of new activities that characterized our traditional worlds. These barriers were not just geographic and economic – they were psychosocial, things like negative reactions to our appearance, loneliness, or dysfunctional or oppressive relationships.

However, it is not just the unwanted limitations and barriers of our traditional worlds that have been removed or minimized. The online revolution has removed, minimized, or altered much of the influence of others, and of many of the conventions, laws, and settings of our traditional worlds. It has enabled us to pursue life relatively unhindered by such influences, and so to live our lives far more on our own terms. As we have seen, there are cases where this transformation has been a disaster, and there are some broader disturbing psychosocial trends. For example, we saw in Sections 2.3.1 (the "daily me" phenomenon), and 2.3.13 ("addiction") that rather than liberating us by opening up realms beyond the limits of our traditional worlds, our use of online worlds may have the opposite effect – namely, leading us to stagnate or shrink by (overly) consolidating and narrowing pre-existing interests and pursuits. And we described in Section 3.3 how aspects of our basic values are lost or marginalized in typical online social worlds.

In one way or another, it has long been recognized that pursuit of life "on your own terms" is a self-defeating way to pursue much that is valuable in life. One classic illustration of the problem is presented in the film *Citizen Kane*,[20] the story of the fall from grace of a great man, setting out to right social injustice in comradeship with similarly motivated friends and colleagues, who is corrupted by his emerging enormous power and influence. The corruption due to this power (as was alleged of Torrentius, the flawed genius described in the Preface)

[20] *Citizen Kane*, RKO Pictures, 1941.

is that Kane comes to regard himself as the sole measure of what is right and good, and the sole arbiter of how to achieve it – even in regard his personal loves.[21] His moral universe, in terms of what is valuable and how to pursue it, becomes something he crafts on his own terms. As Jedediah Leland, Kane's oldest and closest friend, says to him: "The trouble with you Charles is you want love but you want love on your own terms." The tragedy of Kane is given in his reply: "What other terms are there, Jedediah?"

Aristotle also took aim at a similar target by rejecting the idea that one could be self-sufficient in virtue, i.e., someone whose virtue does not depend upon the support and influence of others. His example was the virtue of self-knowledge, and his claim was that we need our close friends if we are to have it: "If, then, it is pleasant to know oneself, and it is not possible to know this without having someone else for a friend, the self-sufficing man will require friendship in order to know himself."[22] So were we to be guided by the idea that we could be self-sufficient in achieving the virtue of self-knowledge, our guidance would necessarily be self-defeating.[23]

---

[21] This is most strikingly captured by his "creation" of Susan Alexander Kane (the sweet, innocent and humble girl who became his mistress and second wife) into a star in ways that became increasingly more demanding, ridiculous, and foreign to her.

[22] Aristotle, *Magna Moralia*, trans. W. D. Ross, Oxford: Clarendon Press, 1915, 1213a20–1213b.

[23] See, Dean Cocking, Aristotle, Friendship and Virtue, *Revue Internationale de Philosophie*, Societe Belge de Philosophie, 2014, 1, pp. 83–90; and Friendship, in *International Encyclopaedia of Ethics*, Oxford: Wiley-Blackwell, 2013. Aristotle is also widely held to require that the virtuous *are* self-sufficient in virtue. Whether this apparent contradiction can be explained away by appeal to different senses of self-sufficiency is not a question we pursue. For a brief discussion of different Aristotelian senses of self-sufficiency that argues Aristotle does not go far enough in recognizing the problems of moral luck for moral character, see Susan Haslip, Aristotle's Theory of the Good Life: A Consideration of the Role of Luck in the Good Life and the Concept of Self-Sufficiency, *Quadlibet Journal*, 5, No. 1, January 2003. See also, Nafsika Athanassoulis, Virtue Ethics, *The Internet Encyclopedia of Philosophy*, www.iep.utm.edu/virtue.

More recently, Martha Nussbaum identifies the driver of having heightened power over one's domain, as one explanation of the objectification of women (by men) that is rampant online.[24] To explain the objectification and shaming of *powerful* women online, she characterizes this driver in terms of Nietzsche's idea of the resentment of the weak toward the powerful. The weak and resentful may spread stories and post images online that objectify and shame the more powerful, and they may do so very easily, across the globe and with anonymity. Thus, online, the weak are able to "fight back" away from the traditional worlds where they are weak and excluded, by creating new worlds online, where they, and not the powerful, hold sway. In the case of men objectifying and shaming female peers, this "revenge of the nerds" is argued to be even more significant. For Nussbaum, anonymity is the key to their freedom to inflict this objectification and hate crime. However, consider how the identity drivers of heightened individual choice and control online (where one is seemingly less subject to the influence and constraints of others and the conditions of one's traditional worlds), play out in different ways, and enable objectification generally across social life online. And while anonymity can be a factor in some cases, often it is not. Commonly, objectification of self, others, and relationships online does not require anonymity, nor even the belief that one is anonymous.

The most obvious objectification online of *self by self* is the reduction of self to the construction of appearances. Indeed, to those appearances constructed by you, seemingly on your own terms. It can be just you, alone, that constructs the story and images of who you are, remarkably absent or dismissive of the influence of others, and the realities of non-virtual worlds that might disrupt the identity

[24] Martha Nussbaum, "Internet Misogyny and Objectification,in *The Offensive Internet*, Cambridge, MA: Harvard University Press, 2010. Objectification, on Nussbaum's account, is presented as a cluster concept involving a variety of ideas. These include treating a person as a tool to one's purposes, lacking in autonomy (as self-determination), lacking agency, being replaceable, lacking subjectivity (and so whose experience and feelings we can ignore), and being reducible to body and appearances.

constructed on one's own terms. And objectification *of others* is ubiquitous on social networking sites: users can treat others instrumentally, deny their subjectivity, reduce one another to appearances and regard each other as replaceable. Just as users are directed to think about themselves as an identity they can construct largely on their own terms, they are also directed to think about their connections to others in this way. Typically, in our traditional social worlds, things are not so unbalanced and extreme.[25]

Self-expression and social connection now represent the dominant uses of the Internet. The main cohort of users are young people. For them, the appeal of being enabled to craft an identity on one's own terms, absent of the influence of others, really has traction. Early mid-teen years onward are precisely the time of significant moves toward separation from parents, and the early days of crafting an identity of one's own more actively and deliberately. Hence, the apparently heightened choice and control over self-expression and social connection provided online is of special interest, truly seductive, to young people. In these early days of crafting identity and relations with others and the world, young people's understanding crucially depends upon what they get from their environment – the prevailing attitudes, judgments, norms, conventions, and rules of the game. Thus, as they increasingly grow up online, they will be especially vulnerable to taking on, or adapting to, the conceptions of self and social connections which online environments present to them. Imagining oneself as able to pursue life on one's own terms, free of the direction and limitations of others and surrounds, is a notable conception conjured up by our online social environments. And this conception is an illusion (a thoroughly and lucratively exploited illusion) of these worlds. It is, as some users have discerned, a "trick," a very good one, a very seductive one, but a trick nonetheless.[26] For example, your teenage son or

[25] It would be laughable to suppose we have no significant experience of living in traditional-world environments where we treat others and ourselves instrumentally and as replaceable. Been to work lately?

[26] See discussions with users in the world of avatars in Tim Guest's excellent book, *Second Lives: A Journey Through Virtual Worlds*, London: Random House, 2008.

brother will tell you (with a straight face) that he has hundreds of friends online. Perhaps he has a thousand. His social networking site will almost certainly also present an extraordinarily skewed vision of who he is – endlessly partying, looking very attractive and pursuing very cool interests. However, having many friends or, even better, some celebrity friends online – as has become the fashion – and being directed to think about yourself through overwhelmingly positive images of your own construction, including ones altogether invented, are not the result of some special ability to choose your own identity unhindered by the influence of others, and the world around you. The contrary is true.

Many young people have hundreds, maybe thousands, of friends online, not because of some (abnormal and offensive) desire for power to overcome their weakness, but more simply (and more reasonably), because they will look like a loser if they do not. It is not hard to understand how this "big numbers" view of friendship got traction. Your connection of easy access to others is now way beyond the confines of the local school or sporting and interest groups. So too then are the associations you can claim. You will, therefore, obviously look like you are not really connected, and so fit for your online-transformed social world, if your numbers resemble anything like what is true in our traditional social worlds. Similarly, where parading celebrities, or important or wealthy people within your "friendship" net has become the rage, you will increasingly be out of the game without them.

So your possibilities have expanded wildly in some ways. You may now have a thousand friends. You may now be far more able to claim celebrity "friends," and to develop and feed desires to have them. But this expansion of possibilities, regarding your desires and how you can meet them, does not mean you are now equipped with heightened capacities for choice and control, and so now enabled to better govern your life on your own terms. Instead, your desires, beliefs and values are being shaped by "what everyone else is doing," and "what everyone else is doing" is being shaped by the design features of your online social world – such as connectivity, isolation, personalisation, recommendation, homophily, positionality and forms of voluntary control over self-expression and presentation. For your alternative is that if you do not, if you fall well short of claiming absurdly large friendship groups, fail to claim any "special" friends, or you are not (at least) self-presenting or promoting as pretty damn happy and successful, then (to these extents) you will be a relative fringe-dweller, not really "in the swim" of your online-transformed social world.

3.5 Online/Offline World Contrasts: Overstated and Alarmist

But perhaps we overstate our case. Recently, for instance, in discussions on the topic of "friendship online," authors (usually those defending the pursuit of friendship online) have noted that current use of social networking sites is mostly (or significantly) about maintaining existing offline friendships. Moreover, the variety of online media available nowadays means that there are also many other "reality" checks that are provided online about the person with whom you are dealing.[27]

In the television series "Catfish," for instance, the truth about the identity of the person doing the catfishing is often uncovered by investigation online. Symmetrically enough, lies and omissions offline can be exposed by investigation online. Many employment applications, for example, have been sunk by something the job applicant published on their social networking site. As we declared in our previous chapters, the Internet is now everywhere and interwoven throughout our everyday lives. Thus, separation between (many) online and offline worlds has largely gone. Accordingly, our story focusing upon the contrasts between them may seem overstated, and so our worries about these contrasts may seem alarmist.

[27] For a good critical discussion, canvassing various ways in which one might object to our approach, see, Sofia Kaliarnta, Using Aristotle's Theory of Friendship to Classify Online Friendships: A Critical Counterview, *Ethics and Information Technology*, 18, no. 2, June 2016, pp. 65–79.

The fact, however, that online and offline worlds are now, and increasingly, interwoven, or that much pursuit of friendship online concerns friendships we have offline, or that we can find out a lot about one another through a variety of online forums, does not undermine the worries we have presented. Online worlds, ever-increasing in kind, are now well embedded in, and ubiquitous across, our traditional worlds. Online worlds may provide some reality checks to both other online worlds and offline worlds, and offline worlds may do so for other offline worlds and online worlds. But whether or not any of this is "winning the day" is very much an open question. Worries about the fate of our plural worlds of public and private life, and the prosocial, basic values they enable, may remain alive and well despite the presence of some "reality checks."

Indeed, what reason is there to think otherwise? We already know from our traditional worlds that psychosocial problems enabled in certain domains commonly creep across others, and that they can flourish despite the presence of resistance and conflicting reality checks in the other domains. So, for example, it is commonplace that one's celebrity in a given domain can spread and impact across one's life generally, and be remarkably resistant to various "reality" checks of other areas, either at a given stage, or at different stages, of one's life. Stories about the negative impact upon real-life and fictional movie stars who are lost to images of their own celebrity abound.[28] And the negative effects on their personal lives plainly often flourish in the face of much resistance and conflicting realities, such as presented by partners, children, friends, or work colleagues. Such problems are also not peculiar to famous people; they abound for "local heroes," such as local sporting stars, high-ranking public servants, academics, or especially good-looking, or wealthy business people.[29]

So why should we think that problems for the fate of prosocial values presented by *online* worlds would fare any better? Not only are

---

[28] See, for example, the classic film noir, *Sunset Boulevard*, Paramount Pictures, 1950. For a "real-life" extreme, see, *Mommie Dearest*, Christina Crawford, William Morrow and Co., 1978.

[29] More on this aspect of the problem of celebrity is presented in Chapter 4.

there obvious reasons to think otherwise, it is hard to see *any* reason to think this. There seems no reason to think that the transmission rate of these problems from online social worlds across other worlds is relatively low, or that the success of antidotes to these problems in online social worlds, such as "reality" checks from some traditional worlds, is relatively high.

3.6 Alarmism about Sexual Predators and Children

One specific example of how some of our fears about online evils have been claimed to be exaggerated and misguided concerns fears of risks to our children from online sexual predators. As we set out in Chapter 1, grooming and sexual predation has proliferated online in both degree and kind. It has been argued, however, that fears about sexual predators attacking our children are overblown. In an article about their extensive study on online predators, Wolak et al[30] offer very interesting and useful evidence about the minds and profiles of online predators and their victims. Contrary to some common fears, they assert that most Internet sex crime does not involve children; that it does not present new forms of sex crime, and that it does not even significantly contribute to the rates of traditional sex crime.[31]So what are we so worried about?

---

[30] Janis Wolak, David Finkelhor, Kimberly J. Mitchell and Michele L. Ybarra Online "Predators" and their Victims: Myths, Realities, and Implications for Prevention and Treatment, *American Psychologist*, February–March, 2008, pp. 111–128.

[31] See, www.unh.edu/ccrc/internet-crimes/Am Psy Paper Highlights.pdf On the "nothing new" point: "Media reports and Internet safety messages about Internet predators often suggest that online meetings between adults and youths that develop into sex crimes constitute a new dimension of child sexual abuse… Although a new medium for communication is involved, the non-forcible sex crimes that predominate as offenses against youths online are not particularly new or uncommon. All states have criminal laws deeming youths below certain ages too young to consent to intercourse." Wolak et al, *Ibid.*, p. 113.

The authors' main concern is to show that online predators mostly prey on the vulnerabilities of our young people, i.e. our teenagers, rather than children, and to then give some account of how and why it is our teens who are most at risk. The main transmission risk, they say, is interactive forums, such as chat-rooms, rather than the posting of personal information on sites like Facebook. Further, it is not young people in general that are at risk, but particular sorts of young people, namely those who have already been abused, neglected or have some other social–psychological problems, and so are already acting out "risky" behaviors *offline*.

Unlike children, young people or teenagers are increasingly immersed in the broader adult community, through school, part-time work and socializing. As emerging adults, young people have limited understanding and practical experience in matters of self-expression and relations with others, and even less in regard to their emerging interests in sex and romance. Yet, at the same time, unlike children, they are increasingly able, interested, and expected to engage in, the broader, adult world. It should be no surprise then, that they turn out to be more at risk than children, and that those who have already suffered abuse or neglect, who are already acting out risky behaviors *offline*, are even more at risk.

But what of the other claims that would contradict our belief in broad-based new risks facing our young people online? We may not be surprised that it is teenagers, especially those who have suffered other significant problems, who are *most* at risk. But if online social worlds are not really contributing to the risks that are already there, and if they are not really contributing new forms of risk, then it would seem that online social worlds do not present risks that are special cause for concern.

First, of course, the focus and findings of this study relate only to sex crime. Other forms of evil online that do not involve sex crime mostly affect young people, and plainly do so in broad-based, new ways. So, even if the authors are right about sex crime online, there is no reason to think (nor any reason to saddle them with the view) that the Internet is not contributing new forms of risk and/or contributing to various traditional forms of risk in other ways, such as with cyberbullying. Second, however, new forms of sex crime and increased sex crime have emerged online.

In fact, in addition to statutory rape, a raft of *new* sex crimes have emerged and been legislated for all over the world – notably online sexual predation and grooming of children and young people. In turn, policing and justice units have sprung up to address these new problems. And sexual crimes online need not get so far as to end up rape. Indeed, online grooming crimes need not even involve any *actual* children or young people at all – much less rape of actual children or young people. Many online predators have been prosecuted as a result of covert operations by police *posing* as children or teenagers.

Grooming is nothing new. Predators have long been grooming children and young people in the physical world – at shopping malls, playing fields, and many other locations. However, the Internet has plainly facilitated the practice in new ways. In addition to the revolution in access and interaction it provides, various conditions of online communication contribute to the blurring and undermining of moral and social understandings, for example, through anonymity, low social transaction costs, atypical control over self-presentation and responsiveness to others, isolation, and the virtuality of the medium. Our teenager is vulnerable to being preyed upon and to being abused in these worlds, not only in ways much less likely to apply to young children, but in ways that do not apply at all to the shopping mall, the playing field or other grooming hot-spots.

Moreover, there is good reason to think that the trend of emerging new crimes and new forms of crime, including sex crime, will continue for some time. As everyone recognizes, new technology is almost always ahead of legislation and the provision of regulatory frameworks to reflect new moral challenges. The Internet presents a monumental case in point since it is constantly and rapidly changing, and has become so dominant across the territory on which we conduct our lives. So new "loopholes" or criminal opportunities should be expected to abound for some time. In addition, the further "twists and turns" of the technology, and its place in our lives, will provide new ways to be vulnerable, and new ways in which otherwise relatively effective guiding moral understandings can be screened off, suspended, and corrupted.

Let us now focus more directly on some of the questions about evil-doing, and about the nature and fate of the moral life, to which we have been led by our investigation into evil online. In the next chapter we begin by developing our account of the moral fog of evil. We do so in counterpoint to other approaches to understanding evil (most notably Hannah Arendt's theory of the "banality of evil"), and by describing and providing an analysis of a variety of ways in which the moral sensibilities, especially of otherwise fairly normal, prosocial people, can be screened off and overturned, both online and in our traditional worlds.

4

The Moral Fog of Our Worlds

So, so you think you can tell
Heaven from Hell, blue skies from pain.
Can you tell a green field from a cold steel rail?
A smile from a veil?
Do you think you can tell?[1]

Pink Floyd

4.1 Introduction

We got the contract for this book over a decade ago (the delay being to the chagrin of ourselves, our publisher, and everyone who knows us). In "those days" there was nothing much around on our topic. On the other hand, the approach of the book then was quite a bit simpler than now, and with the extraordinary rise of social life online since, the original project would have missed much about the contemporary online milieu. Most of all (not that this accounts for the remarkable delay), investigating evil online in the contemporary context of online social worlds increasingly defining social life, has been a goldmine for thinking about wrong and evildoing, how it is enabled to flourish,

[1] Pink Floyd, *A Collection of Great Dance Songs*, "Wish You Were Here," written by David Gilmour and Roger Waters, (Harvest/EMI, U.K.), 1981. For a hilarious take on the problem of moral fog see the comedy sketch 'Nazis', also known as 'Are We the Baddies?', from the British comedy series *That Mitchell and Webb Look*, starring David Mitchell and Robert Webb, British Broadcasting Corporation, 2006.

Evil Online, First Edition. Dean Cocking and Jeroen van den Hoven.

and, as a result, about the nature of moral character and the prosocial life more generally.

We have been led down many tracks, and we have lost our way on more than one or two of them. Mostly, however, the rise of the Internet to so quickly and almost universally provide (or transform) the framework for self-expression and communication within which we conduct our lives, has increasingly and unavoidably led us to consider broader issues concerning the nature of moral character and the prosocial life. In particular, it has led us to focus on how these are created and sustained by the settings of our shared lives, and the milieu of conventions and so forth that we develop in these settings so as to navigate our way through them.

As we said at the outset, our investigation into evil online has led us to be most interested in the various, and sometimes quite atypical, ways in which life online seems to have radically overturned the moral sensibilities of otherwise fairly normal, prosocial people. However, as illustrated by the story of the *Batavia* in our preface, and as evoked by countless other episodes of evil, when we think of the minds of evildoers we commonly conjure up pictures of extreme antisocial attitudes and motives, such as sadism or malice. We imagine minds well beyond the vices and weaknesses most of us share.[2] As Aristotle says of extreme immoralities: "We also use 'bestial' as a term of reproach for people whose vice exceeds the human level."[3]

---

[2] As mentioned in our preface, Kant goes the other way since he thinks we are radically evil in the sense of a propensity for self-conceit (i.e., to place our self-interest above the moral law) that *we all do share*. See, Kant, "Religion within the Boundaries of Mere Reason," *Religion and Rational Theology*, *op. cit.*, (6: 33–34). See also Chapter 5.

[3] Aristotle, NE 114b33. Similarly, Adam Morton describes how we think of evil agency in terms of "diabolical cruelty and of deeply perverse commitment to badness." See Adam Morton, *On Evil: Thinking in Action*, New York: Routledge, 2004, p. 31. There are difficult problems facing how we can attribute blame to these images of evildoers. At least there are if we imagine they do not share our moral understandings, such as that there are powerful reasons against harming innocents. For common views of moral responsibility require a shared account of the reason-giving force of such claims. As Gary Watson explains in relation to Strawson's account of moral responsibility in

We can, however, think of extreme immoralities as informed by a variety of pictures of the minds of evildoers.[4] Moreover, we can think of moral extremes in regard to the practices of a community, or, perhaps, the kinds of injustices that economic or social conditions can present for individuals and communities. Much of our discussion from Chapters 1 and 2 indicates how features of online environments facilitate evildoing, and how they do so by undermining moral understanding about what one is up to, what one is involved in, and what one has become. Our discussions in Chapter 3 on relational aspects of some of our basic values illustrate how dependent our abilities to create and realize these values are upon our location in our traditional plural social worlds, and upon the conventions we have devised over thousands of years for navigating them. These worlds, pre-dating our online-transformed world, not only worked to support our prosocial capacities, they made a suite of important features of our basic values possible.

---

terms of "reactive attitudes": "It is tempting to think that understanding requires a shared framework of values. Can we be in a moral community with those who reject the basic terms of moral community? Are the enemies of moral community themselves members? If we suppose that moral address requires moral community, then some forms of evil will be exempting conditions. If holding responsible requires the intelligibility of moral address, and if a condition of such address is that the other be seen as a potential moral interlocutor, then the paradox results that extreme evil disqualifies one for blame." Gary Watson, "Responsibility and the Limits of Evil: Variations on a Strawsonian Theme," in Gary Watson, Agency and Answerability: Selected Essays, Oxford: Oxford University Press, 2004, pp. 219–259, pp. 233–234. Thanks to Justin Oakley for referring us to Watson. See also Chapter 5.

[4] Similarly, Luke Russell says: "I advocate a restricted conceptual pluralism with regards to evil action. All of us should agree that if an action is evil, it is an extreme culpable wrong, but it is rationally permissible for a person to stipulate that by evil action she will mean malicious and extreme culpable wrong, and rationally permissible for others to stipulate that they will mean defiant extreme culpable wrong, malicious and sadistic extreme culpable wrong, or simply extreme culpable wrong." Luke Russell, *Evil: A Philosophical Investigation*, Oxford: Oxford University Press, 2014, p. 4. Thanks to Justin Oakley for referring us to this passage.

The undermining of moral understanding across all these fronts therefore presents a fundamental kind of evil, and not (just) because it facilitates evildoing. Social and communication worlds that undermine our capacities for appropriate moral understanding thereby undermine our capacity to *be* prosocial, moral beings. Accordingly, such worlds are unjust in a very fundamental way (often to perpetrators as well as victims).[5]

4.2 The Moral Fog of Evil

The term 'moral fog' (or often just the 'fog of…') has been used in some different contexts to describe conditions where normative competence is especially challenged. So, for instance, circumstances in combat and war have sometimes been described as presenting a "fog" or "moral fog" for decision-making due to the environment being especially unpredictable.[6] If, for instance, (to give just one kind of case) it is very difficult to tell combatant from civilian, then it is likewise very difficult to know how to approach and interact with them. The circumstances of it being very difficult to tell friend from foe "fog

[5] One way of seeing this further is in terms of Nancy Snow's recent account of the virtues as important and distinctive forms of what she calls "social intelligence." This, she says: "can be loosely defined as the knowledge, cognitive abilities and affective sensibilities, such as empathy, that enable us to navigate our social world (by) having a well-developed ability to 'read people'…More colloquially, we can describe social intelligence as 'people smarts', and contrast it with academic intelligence, or 'book smarts'". On this approach then, the moral fog would undermine our capacities to be prosocial, moral beings in a fundamental way, since it would undermine the knowledge, cognitive abilities and affective sensibilities that make up the social intelligence of the pro-social, moral life. Nancy E. Snow, *Virtue as Social Intelligence: An Empirically Grounded Theory*, New York: Routledge, 2010, p. 63. Thanks to Justin Oakley for referring us to Snow.

[6] See, for example, the documentary film by Errol Morris, *The Fog of War: Eleven Lessons from the Life of Robert S. McNamara*, USA, 2004.

up" one's relevant decision-making abilities. The term is also sometimes used in spiritual and religious contexts to describe the normative incompetence of our more widely shared and everyday lives, such as often displayed by our pursuit of self-interest, and to cast God or some form of enlightenment as the way forward and out of our fog. In either case, and as we use the term in this book, the "moral fog" describes features or circumstances of our worlds that render the nature and consequences of our conduct opaque, and so undermine our capacities for moral understanding and decision-making.

Highly unpredictable and dangerous combat situations often present very clear examples of such environments. In very different ways, however, so too do our new online-transformed worlds. For here also, our abilities to make and act upon reasonable judgements about our conduct, and about where we are headed, are fogged up in some atypical and hugely amplified ways. Better understanding the features (often the "perfect storm" of features) that enable these problems of moral fog, helps explain much of the explosion in various types of evil that flourish online.

We have seen, for example, how online bullying and harassment are typically not undertaken by evil minds in the sense of minds that understand, and are motivated by, the wrong or evil they do. As we have described, various features of online social or communication environments – such as relative, or seeming, anonymity, the driver of favorable social positioning, the limited/distorted ways of engagement, and the low costs of provoking the reactions of others – assist in inculcating motivational patterns that isolate a person's understanding of what they do from the negative normative force attached to what they do – such as, that I am bullying this person and that this is wrong.

Online social or communication environments can corrupt moral character and agency in online users by allowing them to screen off moral understanding and thereby conceive themselves and their actions as relatively innocuous, using justifications like "it was fun" or "everyone else was doing it". Our cases and trends from Chapters 1 and 3, and our account of morally influential features of online worlds upon living online in Chapter 2, tell a story of how we can be drawn into evil, and into worlds that marginalize and undermine basic values, by a collusion between some of our own needs and limitations, and environments that are not sufficiently rich and functional in addressing them. As indicated, in this chapter we will describe how this collusion sends us astray in our traditional worlds.

The most influential contemporary way in which the evildoing of otherwise relatively prosocial people has been described has been in terms of the banality of evil. Hannah Arendt characterized evil as banal as a result of her coverage of the trial of Adolf Eichmann, the Nazi official responsible for organizing the extermination of Jewish people throughout Europe.[7] Arendt found Eichmann a very unremarkable and ordinary man who quite uncritically accepted, went along with, and carried out with bureaucratic excellence, the mandates of his State.[8] She found him unthinking to the point of largely screening off, or being blind to, the monumental moral horror of the Holocaust he played a key role in deliberately bringing about. His mind, for Arendt, was not motivated by such content as extreme prejudice, malice or hate, but more ordinary, widely shared concerns, such as doing his job well. And she described this, in the last words of her book on the trial, as banal.

The banality of evil has not only been very extensively discussed, the phrase has become common parlance. Most discussion has been about whether evil really is banal, and about what banality really means. At the sharp end, many have rejected the idea altogether. In fact, many have found it offensive. Norman Mailer, for example, described it as superficial, and as a remarkable failure (of liberals generally) to admit the problem of evil minds that can lie behind a facade (or other more genuine expressions) of normality, ordinariness and dullness.[9] Certainly

---

[7] See Hannah Arendt, *Eichmann in Jerusalem: A Report on the Banality of Evil*, *op. cit.*; and Raul Hilberg, *The Destruction of the European Jews*, 1st ed. Chicago: Quadrangle Books, 1961.

[8] In an oft-cited quote one court physician also struck by the apparent ordinariness of Eichmann said: "He seems remarkably normal. At least a lot more normal than I am after examining him."

[9] See, for example, an interview with Mailer, *Norman Mailer: The Sanction to Write*, www.youtube.com/watch?v=FhRCbRXWBdo (accessed 21 January 2017).

Mailer is right that evil minds can coexist with the ordinary. As noted in Chapter 3 (and will be mentioned later), they can do so due to the plurality of our identities – so, for example, one may be kind in one domain, but ruthless in another – and, of course, a cloak of civility commonly provides cover to obscure evil.[10] And since all of this has long been fairly obvious, it would be remarkably unimaginative to take appearances of ordinariness or normality in an evildoer to mean that the mind that lay behind these appearances was likewise.

On the other hand, Arendt was not guilty of failing to admit the reality of evil minds, in the sense of motivating attitudes of extreme ill-will.[11] She just did not think it applied to the monumental evildoing of Eichmann. And, of course, she had a much bigger story about totalitarianism and how it dominates and encourages unthinking, banal evildoers. Nevertheless, she may well have been wrong about Eichmann, and Mailer well have been right in describing her

---

[10] In recent years, for instance, the world was shocked by two separate cases of Austrian men, both engineers, who had built secret rooms in their houses where they had each kept captive a young girl who they serially raped. Both men were also quite active, and in some ways well-respected, members of their community. In each case the "double life" had gone on for over a decade. These are the cases of Joseph Fritzl and Franz Prikopil. More recently, there was the similar case of Ariel Castro in Cleveland, Ohio. The secret life of Dennis Rader had even more longevity. Rader was an active Lutheran, an ex-Boy Scout leader, married to the same woman for more than 30 years, and had two children and a seemingly functional normal social and family life in Wichita, Kansas. In 2005 however, he confessed to being a serial killer. He confessed to being the self-described BTK – acronym for "Bind, Torture, Kill" – who was responsible for at least ten sadistic random murders. These murders were conducted over the entire period of his seemingly "civil" married and family life. A life that spanned over more than 30 years and also involved significant religious and community service. See, Roy Wenzl, Tim Potter, L. Kelly and Hurst Laviana, *Bind, Torture, Kill: The Inside Story of BTK the Guy Next Door*, New York: HarperCollins Publishers, 2007.

[11] As Alan Norrie says and quotes from Arendt: "Arendt saw that many Nazis acted out of a deep "hatred and resentment against all those who were better off than themselves, and who now…were in their power." Alan Norrie, "The Scene and the Crime: Can Critical Realists Talk about Good and Evil?," *Journal of Critical Realism*, 11, no. 1, pp. 76–93 (2012), p. 90. For the Arendt quote see, Hannah Arendt, *Origins of Totalitarianism*, London: Harcourt Brace, 1968, p. 454.

judgment (of Eichmann's apparent banality) as fairly superficial and unimaginative.

Most recently, for example, in *Eichmann Before Jerusalem*,[12] Bettina Stangneth argues, on the basis of very detailed research and significant historical evidence on the life and activities of Eichmann (before Jerusalem), that he put on a show at his trial and was quite successful in deceiving observers – including Arendt. Contrary to his act of being merely a simple obedient civil servant, an instrument and cogwheel in the Nazi machinery, Stangneth persuasively casts him as a very strong believer in the Nazi ideology who actively thought through and very much identified with, indeed was very proud of, what the ideology implied, and not just required, but enabled, him to do.[13]

The "banality of evil" therefore, may well be based on a historical mistake – although it is often regarded as one of the more influential and important moral philosophical ideas of the twentieth century.[14] Whether Stangneth is right or not, Arendt's notion of the banality of evildoing, and how this is enabled by totalitarian regimes, might

---

[12] Bettina Stangneth, *Eichmann Before Jerusalem: The Unexamined Life of a Mass Murderer*, (translated by Ruth Martin), New York: Alfred A Knopf, 2014. Many, before Stangneth, had rejected Arendt's picture of Eichmann. See, in particular, David Cesarani, *Becoming Eichmann: Rethinking the Life, Crimes and Trial of a "Desk Murderer*," Cambridge, MA: Da Capo Press, 2006.

[13] See, for example, Steven Aschheim's review of Stangneth's book, *The New York Times*, Sunday Book Review, 4 December 2014. So, for instance, he says of Eichmann: "Throughout his post-1945 exile he remained a passionate, ideologically convinced National Socialist. He proudly signed photos with the title 'Adolf Eichmann—SS Obersturmbannführer (retired)' and, quite unlike a plodding functionary, boasted of his 'creative' work. At one point he described the mass deportation of more than 400,000 Hungarian Jews as his innovative masterpiece: 'It was actually an achievement that was never matched before or since.'"

[14] See, for example, Susan Neiman, *Evil in Modern Thought: An Alternative History of Philosophy*, Princeton, NJ: Princeton University Press, 2002.

nevertheless be thought still to be an important one.[15] Certainly, at the least, Arendt's account of Eichmann as moved by fairly mundane motives, and unthinking about the horror of his conduct, is hardly unique as a characterization of some of the evildoers of Nazi Germany (and so there is quite a bit of independent support for this approach). Sarah Helm, for example, who conducted extensive research and interviews with survivors of Ravensbruck – the only Nazi concentration camp for women – describes many of the female guards very much in this way, i.e., as ordinary people without criminal records who became guards for mundane reasons such as the salary, security and position, but who nevertheless often, very quickly and easily, also became evildoers.[16]

Stangneth's portrayal of Eichmann, and how he deployed a range of means to plausibly deny, frame and make his role seem innocuous, does, in any case, provide a striking example of how interpretive flexibility (as described in Chapter 2) can be exploited. Eichmann was able to give his actions the appearance of obedience to superiors and naiveté, hence relative innocence, by exploiting the interpretive flexibility embodied in this complex historical episode in history. This is what Hans Lada, the sadistic and efficient SS Colonel played by Christoph Waltz in Quentin Tarantino's *Inglourious Basterds*, attempted to do when things fell apart for the Nazis and he was captured. Of course, unlike Eichmann, in Tarantino's tale Lada's spin on his role didn't impress too many people.[17] Many of the protagonists that we describe also help themselves to descriptions that frame their conduct as relatively innocent. Mostly, however, our protagonists are not dissembling when they do so. Instead, they really believe, for example, that "it was just a joke," or that they were "just doing what everyone else was doing."

---

[15] See, for example, Alan Norrie, *op. cit.*, pp. 89–90; Paul Formosa, "Moral Responsibility for Banal Evil," *Journal of Social Philosophy*, 37, no. 4, Winter 2006, pp. 503–504, pp. 501–520.

[16] See, Sarah Helm, *If this is a Woman. Inside Ravensbruck: Hitler's Concentration Camp for Women*, London: Little, Brown, 2014.

[17] *Inglourious Basterds* (A Band Apart, The Harvey Weinstein Company, Universal Pictures), 2009.

The main reasons that have led some to reject Arendt's view have been that her account seems to let evildoers like Eichmann off the hook, and fail to capture the evilness of the mind from which evil acts spring.[18] It lets evildoers off the hook since (for many) an evildoers' lack of understanding of the moral qualities of their conduct seems to mean that they cannot be held morally responsible. And it falls short of capturing the nature of evildoing, since (for many) evildoing requires agency from an evil mind in the sense of a mind that aims at the harm.

Our account of the moral fog of evil might well be thought to face much the same objections. Since we think (much) evildoing is undertaken by people who otherwise may be relatively prosocial and normal, and who do not clearly understand, much less intend, their conduct as evil, our approach may also seem to fall foul of both standard accounts of responsibility and evil. We address these concerns ahead, in Section 5.4, "Evil and Responsibility". Our main reason for moving away from Arendt's view is that while, as we have certainly seen, many cases of evildoing seem banal, often the evildoing is not. Often there is much more to be said that helps explain how

[18] See, for example, Joseph Beatty, "Thinking and Moral Considerations: Socrates and Arendt's Eichmann," *The Journal of Value Inquiry*, 10, no. 1, Winter, 1976, pp. 266–278. Beatty argues that Arendt casts Eichmann as a moral idiot to whom we cannot attribute moral responsibility. Other writers have made similar arguments. Formosa's article (*op. cit.*) led us to these discussions, and is very helpful generally in characterizing and referencing a range of such attacks on Arendt's view, and for providing a good defence illustrating how Arendt's Eichmann can be understood to be morally responsible. The defense, like most, is in terms of the evildoer having the relevant capacities for the thinking required for moral understanding, even though they may not exercise them during the time of their evil conduct. We discuss this "tracing" approach to moral responsibility for wrong and evildoing more in Section 5.4, "Evil and Responsibility." See also, David Cesarani, *Eichmann: His Life and Crimes*, London: Vintage, 2004; Todd Calder's discussion, "The Apparent Banality of Evil: The Relationship between Evil Acts and Evil Character," *Journal of Social Philosophy*, 34, no. 3, Fall 2003, pp. 364–376.

banal attitudes and desires, in the sense of mundane, widely shared ones, get traction.[19] Evil that is guided by mundane and widely shared attitudes and motives need not depict (against how the description of the banality of evil has always been understood to apply) a mind that is monumentally unthinking.[20]

---

[19] Of course, as we have mentioned, Arendt also thought there was much more to say about how banal attitudes get traction. Her focus was on the impact of totalitarianism. As we note later, our focus is much broader, highlighting a range of features conducive to moral fog, including cases where the evildoing is not banal in the sense of extraordinarily unthinking (and also where the motives may not be banal, such as evildoing done from extreme hate or malice).

[20] In Section 4.3, for instance, we draw attention to widely shared learning vulnerabilities, and to some (reasonable) demands of self-interest in "us and them" circumstances. In these cases, one's motives may well be banal (as mundane and unsurprising) but one need not be monumentally morally unthinking in the sense of being unable to think from the standpoint of another, or unable to put oneself in the shoes of another. One's failures of moral understanding also need not be *extraordinarily* below what we might reasonably expect of someone in the circumstances. Writers on evil commonly require that evil has no justification or excuse sufficient to justify or excuse the evildoing (see, for example, Claudia Card, mentioned in our discussion in Section 5.4, "Evil and Responsibility"). This, of course, is true. If we can be excused, then we are not responsible for evildoing, and if we are justified, then (overall, at least), we have done something permissible or right. But one can have, say, an excuse, such as widely shared learning vulnerabilities, that gives *some* excuse. It may not win the day. It may not suffice to get one off the hook. But it may nevertheless be a genuine excuse. It need not be mere "spin." If one is to be held culpable for evildoing, then there must have been something else one should have done, and so in some sense (for most) something else one could have done. But one's failure to do this "something else," such as not continuing to simply trust the directions of elders, mentors, and experts, need not be due to an inability to think from the standpoint of someone else. It may, for example, simply be due to a failure to recognize the limits and pitfalls of trusting elders and so on – namely, that, in all sorts of ways, such trust can also lead one terribly astray regarding how to treat (certain) others. Of course, the limits and pitfalls of such trust has the consequence that one may well not get the standpoint of these others right. But thinking more about their standpoint need not help. The problem is that *how* to think about their standpoint has been sent astray and often not without some justification or excuse.

Understanding evildoing in terms of banality seemed to gain significant support from perhaps the most famous experiment undertaken in social psychology. In 1961, within a year of Eichmann's trial, Stanley Milgram, professor of psychology at Yale University, who was intrigued by the trial and the Nazi experience generally, devised and conducted an experiment in which the subjects were told that they were participating in an experiment about learning and memory. Under instructions from the experimenter they were to act as "teachers" by asking questions of someone (who was, in some of the experimental conditions, out of their view) and administering "electric shocks" to the person whenever they made a mistake. Moreover, these electric shocks were, as the instructor directed, to be increased with each mistake. Of course, there were no real electric shocks, the "learner" was not a fellow subject but acting their part in the experiment, and the experiment was not about learning and memory but, rather, to determine how far people would go when an authority figure ordered them to harm others. Incredibly (seemingly), the majority of subjects continued to give "shocks" to the "learner" up to very high levels – levels that were labelled as increasingly severe on the mock "shock-meter" in the experiment. Some 65 % of subjects continued to give electric shocks until the maximum possible level – "danger – severe shock."[21]

Between Milgram and Arendt, the banality of evildoing became a major theme in social psychology.[22] Driven by Milgram's evidence and Arendt's analysis, the paradigm shift claimed that people's moral failures or evil conduct did not necessarily stem from bad or evil

[21] Various discussions qualify and reject these figures and much of Milgram's study and claims. For an interesting critical account that rejects the legitimacy of Milgram's experiments, see, Gina Perry, *Behind the Shock Machine: The Untold Story of the Notorious Milgram Psychology Experiments*, Brunswick (Victoria): Scribe, 2012, and (Revised Edition) New York: The New Press, 2013.

[22] In addition to the oft-cited influence of the Nazi experience, Milgram also had Solomon Asch as his PhD supervisor at Harvard, who, a decade earlier, produced some ground-breaking work on the conformity effect of group pressure. See also our section ahead, "Keeping up with Others."

moral character. Rather, evildoers may be of normal character, and their fall or leap into evildoing the result of certain features of their circumstances, in particular, the influence of authority figures, and their uncritical acceptance of such influence.

In 1971, Philip Zimbardo, professor of psychology at Stanford University, carried out another famous experiment. The basement of the psychology department had been set up as a mock prison and students, chosen for their generally prosocial and morally healthy attitudes, were to stay there for two weeks playing the roles of prison guards and prisoners. The experiment had to be shut down in six days due to the rapid rise in antisocial and abusive behaviour. Unlike Milgram's experiment, the subjects knew they were just role-playing and they were not directed by the authority figure (here Zimbardo) to harm others. Nevertheless, neither of these factors seemed to slow them down very much. Once into playing their roles they soon came up with appalling behaviour all by themselves. In an overview of his book about the experiment, *The Lucifer Effect: Understanding How Good People Turn Evil*, Zimbardo describes the banality of evil quite broadly: "as everyman and every woman's potential for engaging in evil deeds despite their generally moral upbringing and prosocial life style."[23]

From Milgram, Zimbardo and many other social science experiments, various conditions have been identified as important to understanding how otherwise normal, prosocial, people, can apparently be so unthinking and lacking in moral imagination. Representative of the views of most, Zimbardo describes some of the main conditions:

> In a situation that implicitly gives permission for suspending moral values, many of us can be morphed into creatures alien to our usual natures.... Some of the necessary ingredients are: diffusion of responsibility, anonymity, dehumanization, peers who model harmful behavior, bystanders who do not intervene, and a setting of power differentials.[24]

[23] See "Overview" http://www.lucifereffect.com/index.html (accessed 05 February, 2018). See also Philip Zimbardo, *The Lucifer Effect: Understanding How Good People Turn Evil*, New York: Random House, 2007.

[24] "Power Turns Good Soldiers in to Bad Apples," Philip G. Zimbardo, *The Boston Globe*, 9 May 2004.

Across the varieties of evildoing where the values of ordinary people are suspended in some sense, while not all of these conditions are necessary, many are often present. There is however, much more to consider, both about these features, and about other wellsprings for evildoing. And there is much more to add to the story of seemingly banal evildoing. Our accounts in Section 4.3 of evildoing undertaken in a moral fog aims to help this further consideration. First, however, let us begin developing our story of the moral fog, and how it contributes to understanding evildoing, especially by otherwise fairly normal prosocial people, by considering another very common description of the moral psychology of wrong and evildoing – namely, cognitive dissonance.

Along with the "banality of evil," this description is also commonly applied to the wrong and evildoing of otherwise relatively normal people. Evildoers who have already abandoned or overturned (appropriate) moral understandings are obviously not the best candidates for being understood as in a state of cognitive dissonance about their bad conduct. To be in a state of cognitive dissonance is to think one's conduct permissible/righteous, but also, at the same time, recognize there is something bad or wrong about it. It is to be in some state of conflict about the permissibility of what one is up to. However, those already extremely antisocial evildoers, who have left behind their "better angels" are, therefore, not wrestling with them. How, then, does thinking in terms of moral fog add anything to, or move away from, picturing the wrong and evildoing of otherwise fairly normal people in terms of cognitive dissonance?

While, of course, we don't have any reason to deny the phenomenon of cognitive dissonance, many of the cases of wrong and evildoing online we have canvassed are striking precisely because of the apparent lack of any cognitive dissonance. Descriptions such as "it was fun," "it's just a post on an online site," "everyone is doing it," "it's virtual (not real), its fantasy, its play," "because we could," and so on, suggest a moral psychology where appropriate moral understanding has been screened off – and so not thought to (so much) apply – by features of the agent's settings and milieu. Thus, instead of the person's conduct being seen (by them) as a problem, and so, as on the cognitive dissonance scenario, in need of justification or excuse, those involved do not see much of a need for justification or excuse. Recall, for instance, some of our "pranksters" from Chapter 1, such as Roman Atwood who was very proud of giving the world "stuff to talk about," and who cast himself as some kind of alluring enigma.

It was these kinds of cases that first led us to think of evildoers as in a moral fog, where appropriate moral understandings are "screened from view" so that conduct that is evil no longer seems a moral issue. Or, just as convincingly, where the person's guiding moral framework is "fogged up," not so much because it has been screened from view, but rather, because, in the circumstances, it has been turned on its head. Thus, what was obviously bad, now seems fine. Either way, the descriptor of "cognitive dissonance" has little application to such cases. On the other hand, while the descriptor of the "banality of evil" can apply to many (though far from all) cases where moral understanding has been screened from view, or inverted, and where they may be little cognitive dissonance, it provides little explanatory value.[25] We now develop our case for this throughout the next section, the main concern of which is to illustrate how various features of our lives bring about varieties of moral fog, and to show how seeing things this way does help explain a range of cases of wrong and evildoing.

4.3 The Shared Life and Our Vulnerability to Evil

In a chilling series of interviews with ten farmers who had become mass murderers in the daily killing sprees of Rwanda, Jean Hatzfeld, in his book *Machete Season: The Killers of Rwanda Speak*[26], paints a vivid picture of one of the extreme contemporary cases of evildoing.

---

[25] As we have noted, we are not suggesting that Arendt, or her followers, mistakenly imagined that the description had much explanatory value. As noted, for Arendt, it was the impact of totalitarianism that did the explanatory work, i.e., that gave traction to evildoing from banal motives. Our move is to claim a much broader explanation (in terms of a variety of features that bring about moral fog) and to argue the case by showing how it applies to, and helps explain, a wide range of cases of evildoing (including both cases of evildoing that can be described as banal, and cases that cannot).

[26] Jean Hatzfeld, *Machete Season: The Killers in Rwanda Speak*, New York: Farrar, Straus, Giroux, 2005/Picador, 2006.

These farmers, who seemingly easily and quickly became mass murderers, did not need anonymity to provide much-needed cover for their evil. Rather, their turn to evil flourished under instructions from local authorities, with much support from their community and those close to them, and alongside the continuation of their otherwise very ordinary, domestic, and even good, lives.

As one of the farmers-turned-mass murderer put it:

'Some offenders claim that we changed into wild animals… that we were blinded by ferocity. That is a trick to sidetrack the truth. I can say this: outside the marshes, our lives seemed quite ordinary. We sang on the paths… we had our choice amid abundance. We chatted about our good fortune, we soaped off our bloodstains in the basin, our noses enjoyed the aromas of full cooking pots. We rejoiced in the new life about to begin by feasting on leg of veal. We were hot at night atop our wives, and we scolded our rowdy children. …We put on our field clothes. We swapped gossip at the cabaret, we made bets on our victim, spoke mockingly of cut girls, squabbled foolishly over looted grain. We sharpened our tools on whetting stones. We traded stories about desperate Tutsi tricks, we made fun of every "Mercy!" cried by someone who'd been hunted down, we counted up and stashed away our goods.'[27]

[27] We were led to Hatzfeld's book (where we first found this quote) on reading an excellent essay by Michael Massing "Trial and Error," in *The New York Times*, Sunday Book Review, 17 October 2004. Many of the tales in Hatzfeld's book are not for the faint-hearted. The killing of mothers with babies, children and old friends, and how these killings were undertaken are horrific. There are stories, for instance, of fathers teaching their young sons how to use the machete – sometimes on the bodies of those already killed, sometimes on live people who had been captured – and of how the boys would mostly "practice" on other young children because of their relatively similar size. And they are horrific in their ordinariness (or perhaps, in the corruption of being able to be ordinary that they illustrate – being able, for example, to trust, and so fairly uncritically follow the lead of local authorities, community elders, and the support of, otherwise functional, vibrant family and social lives). Recently, also, Arne Johan Vetlesen has argued that being a part of a larger historical narrative of victimhood is a key factor in much collective evildoing, and that this feature importantly distinguishes collective evildoing from individual evildoing. See, Arne Johan Vetlesen, *Evil and Human Agency: Understanding Collective Evildoing*, Cambridge: Cambridge University Press, 2006. Thanks to Justin Oakley for this point and reference.

Many of the Rwandan farmers reported how easily they were able to trade their daily routine of using machetes to fell crops for the daily routine of using machetes to fell Tutsi. In this, and many other (less extreme) cases like it, we and our immediate community support and legitimize our conduct by understanding and describing what we do in overwhelmingly neutral and positive terms – such as, for example, "They deserved it"; "It was my job"; "It's just business"; or, in the age of the Internet, "It was just a posting on a website."[28] There is a large variety of such more palatable descriptions and their influence and credibility is importantly enhanced by a surrounding community that is otherwise relatively ordinary, even prosocial and morally valuable, and so otherwise a relatively functional community. Together our legitimizing claims and our otherwise quite ordinary and functional prosocial lives create a moral fog obscuring recognition of what we do and what we have become.[29] In this way, our descent in to evildoing is enabled by, and very close to, our ordinary, relatively prosocial lives.

---

[28] In a case that received world-wide publicity in late April 2010, a man who went to the aid of a woman being attacked in New York was himself then fatally stabbed. The Good Samaritan lay dying for almost two hours with more than twenty people passing by who did nothing to help. This phenomenon is not new. There have been many cases, both real and experimental, that show that people often fail to help when they could seemingly do so fairly easily. In this case, however, one man did stop. He stopped long enough to use his mobile to record the man dying so that he could then post the footage on the Internet. Cases like this, of allowing harm for file-sharing purposes, are now quite common – recall also the "doing harm" cases of "happy slapping" mentioned in Chapter 1.

[29] Morton distinguishes between the attractiveness of evil itself (which may be very hard to understand) and the attractive power of images of evil (which may be not so hard to understand). So, e.g., while there have long been serial killers, in more recent times, anyone involved in serial killing is very likely to think of themselves as a serial killer and be conscious of the popular images that have been attached to the label. And aspects of these images are much easier to understand as being attractive to people than is the demonic image of, say, the sadistic torturer. And, as Morton notes, "the less real the psychological insight that comes with the image the better it can serve this role… The more the image represents an actual personality the harder it is to identify with the image unless one does in fact have that personality.," *On Evil*, *op. cit.*, p. 32.

A study on the long-term effects of Nazi propaganda on children who grew up in Germany under the Third Reich, provides an illustrative example.[30] The study not only found Nazi propaganda to have been incredibly effective on children and young people,[31] but also that the impact of the "brainwashing" on the children could last a lifetime, and that the impact was most pronounced in areas that were already quite anti-Semitic, i.e., where a "supportive" environment for such views already existed. One of the leaders of the research team, Hans-Joachim Voth, said of his study:

> It's not just that Nazi schooling worked, that if you subject people to a totalitarian regime in their formative years it will influence the way their mind works. The striking thing is that it doesn't go away afterward (and)… The extent to which Nazi schooling worked depended crucially on whether the overall environment where children grew up was already a bit anti-Semitic.[32]

Our children are now born in to online worlds. Worlds that have brought problems of moral fog, where normalizing and legitimizing influences enable evil to flourish, in ways never seen and otherwise hardly imagined. We can (as noted much earlier) all now, quite literally, eat our cereal or relax in our bed while watching killings, including gruesome executions and torture, or violent or child pornography. Our teenagers routinely, and often in extreme ways, come under attack from bullies or predators in their own bedrooms. In fact, on our desktop, or the mobile in our hand, we all have access to an abundance of fraud, theft, blackmail, threats, bullying, manifestations of terrorism, acts of pedophilia, sexual violence, pornography, child predation, all other sorts of violence, including murder and sadistic harm, self-destructive and "hate" communities, pseudoscience and all

[30] Nico Voigtlander and Hans-Joachim Voth, "Taught to Hate: Nazi Indoctrination and anti-Semitic beliefs in Germany," *Proceedings of the National Academy of Sciences, USA*, 112, no. 26, 2015, pp. 7931–7936.

[31] So, for instance, anti-Semitic attitudes were found to be far more widespread and extreme among those who grew up as children under the reign of the Third Reich, than among those who grew up before or after.

[32] See, https://www.rt.com/news/267550-nazi-propaganda-germany-children (accessed 21 November 2017).

kinds of gross indecency. Moreover, as we argued in Chapter 3, many of us increasingly live in online social worlds where the demolition of public/private contrasts has taken with it important features of some of our basic prosocial values. And all of this carries on within the normalcy of surrounds provided by our homes, offices, schools or cafes, and our shared lives with family, friends and at work.

Many are outraged if attempts are made to bring, say, a porn store or a poker machine venue, in to their traditional geographic neighborhood ("not in my backyard" concerned citizens commonly protest). Not so many, however, are likewise outraged by the fact that they have these things at home on the desktop in their teenager's bedroom, or on the mobile phone their teenager rarely puts down. And as with the conclusion of the study by Voth et al., it seems reasonable to expect that the varied negative impacts of growing up online upon the moral understanding of our young people will be long-lasting.

In our traditional, everyday domestic worlds, before the online revolution, many of the cases of evil conduct and attitudes we have seen would have been recognized plainly as the expression of a mental illness, or of self-destructive, criminal intentions or wicked communities. Our recognition of the evil involved in our relatively new online worlds is clouded by a cluster of features of online environments (as set out in Chapter 2) that frame the way the technology enables us to communicate. Thus, as we have suggested, one important reason why online bullies typically have limited understanding of the evil they do is that, unlike traditional worlds, they typically do not have to see, engage with or respond to much of the damage done to those they bully. The technology brings a moral fog of its own that puts moral dialogue at arm's length.[33]

[33] This is not to deny that many trolls, also "get off" on such reactions and on seeing the damage they do. Thanks to Justin Oakley for putting this point to us. As we say throughout, and address more directly in Section 5.4, "Evil and Responsibility," we do not, of course, imagine that our account of the morally fogged up mind altogether replaces more traditional pictures of evil minds in terms of a mind that well understands the evil they do, and perhaps even aims at it. We are pluralists about evil minds. We do think, however, that the "fogged up" mind is more often in action than most of us normally think. Our effort to illustrate (and so convince you of) this, is presented by our descriptions of a broad range of ways (mostly quite common, widely shared, and – once said out loud – easily recognized) in which moral fog can come about.

Sometimes, the way we understand things in our traditional worlds can clear up the moral fog in our online worlds. So, for example, parents may discover and address the bullying engaged in by their teenage daughter online. Just as likely, of course, they may not. First, it was a great deal easier to be a parental monitor and guide to your children in their relations with the outside world when there was only one phone at home, usually in the "family space" of a lounge-room or hallway. Second, even if the parent does discover the problem it can be difficult to address. The dominance of living online has brought with it significant new obstacles, such as, for example, that one's teenager's entire social world might be at stake. And third, the parent may well observe the bullying but not quite recognize it as such and so not provide appropriate parental guidance, because they, too, are caught up in moral fog online.[34]

Many of our cases of evildoing, both online and in traditional worlds, will seem striking examples of the banality of evil. Many of them are, at least in terms of the attitudes and motives of the perpetrators. However, moral fog, or some of its many varieties, helps explain the banality. So, for example, among the many and varied cases of online bullying, banal attitudes (attitudes that are mundane and commonplace) such as "it was fun" or "because I could," feature prominently. But if you were not already disposed, for example, from some mental illness, or antisocial or immoral attitudes, then why would you think that "because it was fun" or "because I could" sufficed to give you a reason for evildoing?[35] How could you be so unthinking and morally blind?

We still want to understand how the unthinking moral blindness comes about, and what we might do about it. Certainly, for example, if we are parents of online bullies we will have such concerns. We will want answers to: "Well, if you didn't think you had any reason to do

[34] The early case of Megan Meier seems to provide a spectacular example.

[35] Again, as we have said, along with Mailer, the reason it may not suffice may simply be because such descriptions are mere appearances masking far more antisocial attitudes and desires. As we have made plain, however, many cases are not like this.

what you did, how could you be so unthinking?" "You are not a bad person, right, so are you a complete idiot?" As we have seen, often online bullying is not driven by minds that are especially antisocial or stupid. The moral fog of online communication due to not having to see, engage with or respond to much of the impact of and reactions to those whom one bullies, helps explain how such wrong and evildoing may flourish under the influence of banal attitudes.[36]

There are many kinds of moral fog. A variety of features of our own nature, of our shared lives with others, and of the settings within which we conduct them, help explain different kinds of moral fog and the wrong, bad and evildoing it enables. Zimbardo's list of features conducive to evildoing – notably, diffusion of responsibility, anonymity, dehumanization, peers who model harmful behavior, bystanders who do not intervene, and a setting of power differentials – are all conducive to moral fog, and we have seen their application in many of our cases. But, as we have indicated, there is much more to say, both about these features and other considerations. Let us begin with an especially clear case.

You see a picture of a proud father with his arm around his son. The boy has done well in his end of year high school exams. The boy is beaming, obviously very happy with himself. What do you see?

You see a young boy, excited to have done well, and the way that he is appreciated by his father for doing so. Your reactions will be: "What a good boy, excited about doing well, and what a good father supporting and rewarding his son for doing so"…"I'm lucky my father was like that"… "I wish my father was more like that" and so on. Such reactions reflect your understanding of the importance of the shared life between parents and children to functional moral formation.

In the next picture, you again see a proud father with his arm around his young son. This time, however, they are both wearing Ku Klux Klan regalia. They are members attending a KKK function. They are not wearing the hoods, so you can again see that the boy is

---

36 See also, Section 5.5, "Nothing new under the sun," for more on the changing nature of bullying in our online-transformed worlds.

beaming and very happy with himself. So what do you see now? This time you see how a boy may be "turned bad" by a father who perverts his role as a moral guide to his son. Your reactions will be of the kind: "What chance does this boy have?"... "How could a father raise his son to discriminate and hate?" and so on. This time your reactions reflect your recognition of the dysfunctional impacts parents can have upon their children.

In the case of parents' effects on children, the impact upon moral formation is obvious to most of us. And often enough, as in this case, we have mixed and conflicting reactions (usually less extreme ones) since such pictures are of the same parent and child. There are, however, a variety of ways in which our moral formation, for better or worse, continues to be fundamentally dependent upon our shared lives with others well beyond when we are young. The ways in which this is so are also fairly obvious once said out loud. Nevertheless, they are routinely missed by many contemporary accounts of how people turn bad. Consider, for example, an extension of this kind of need and limitation of our nature – our dependence upon superiors, elders, and mentors – that seems important to what is going on in our social science experiments discussed above.

4.3.1 Learning and Development Vulnerabilities

Our education, moral or otherwise, fundamentally depends upon the guidance we get from parents, elders, experts or mentors. Our learning and conduct within areas with which we are relatively unfamiliar needs navigational help from those who do have experience, understanding and so some authority. Accordingly, when professors at Ivy League universities direct or permit us to do bad things in the name of important experiments in social science we will be inclined to take their lead. We will be inclined toward relatively uncritical acceptance of their orders and permissions.

Many writers have claimed that these experiments show how easily we will throw away the dictates of conscience in the face of conflicting directions or permissions from authority. In a representative statement, Velasquez (et al.) say:

> In view of the Milgram experiments, the Nazi crimes are not difficult to understand. Milgram himself suggested that one of the major factors accounting for the Holocaust was the ready propensity of human beings to obey authorities even when obedience is wrong. Indeed, although Milgram's experiment has been repeated dozens of times with many different groups of people, the results are always the same: most people will obey external authority over the dictates of conscience.[37]

The problem, however, is not so much that we will so easily throw away the dictates of conscience. Rather, it is that the dictates of conscience, especially in areas with which we are unfamiliar, we largely get from those who do have far more expertise and authority.

Electrocuting or abusing someone may normally seem very wrong, but our authorities are world-class experts at some of the best universities in the world. The influence of their authority, and our relatively uncritical acceptance is not really banal, in the sense of some monumental moral unthinkingness that so easily, and from mundane motives, becomes commonplace. For the relatively uncritical acceptance is, in some large part, driven by the needs and limits of our learning, namely, our need to have guidance to appreciate and navigate unfamiliar worlds by those more expert. And so, when they lead us astray or trick us, they play on our learning vulnerabilities to create a moral fog about what we do, which in turn enables our evildoing.

Consider, for example, Jane Elliott's famous "blue-eyed/brown-eyed" experiments. Elliott first conducted her experiments in Riceville, Iowa, when she was the teacher of third-graders in the late 1960s. Directly in the wake of the assassination of Reverend Martin Luther King, she wanted to get across to the children (all white) what the prejudice and discrimination of racism would be like. She filmed one of her early exercises with her class and it is easily found for viewing online. She told the children that blue-eyed people were better and smarter than brown-eyed people and divided the class in to those with blue eyes and those with brown. The brown-eyed children were

[37] Manuel Velasquez, Claire Andre, Thomas Shanks, S.J., and Michael J. Meyer, "Conscience and Authority," Markkula Centre for Applied Ethics, Ethics Resources, 1 December 1988.

made to wear identifying collars (put on by those with blue-eyes) and were not to play with the blue-eyed children – they would be segregated and discriminated against.

Very soon things went pear-shaped. As Elliott described at the time, cooperative, good children became vicious, cruel and discriminatory within 15 minutes. Zimbardo rightly notes that Elliott's experiment provides a striking example of the influence teachers may have in shaping the reality of their students. Similarly, of course, this is important to the experiments of both Milgram and Zimbardo. It is also, like Zimbardo's "prison experiment," a clear example of the power of "us and them" conditions where, being "one of them" rather than "one of us," is to be dumb, bad, inferior and so on. Reasonable demands of self-interest recommend avoiding damnation. So, again, it is not really a case of the banality of evil (as "monumentally morally unthinking," although certainly it is as "unsurprising," or as "stating the obvious") to cling on to being "one of us," to avoid being "one of them," and to be resentful and hostile about it if unable to do so.

Elliott turned the tables for the children in repeating the experiment, so that those with brown eyes would now be favored. For the most part the brown-eyed children then repeated the discrimination on those who had done it to them. Zimbardo notes this seems surprising – not so good news perhaps for moral character – since we might hope that those who have been at the sharp end of abusive discrimination would therefore understand well what is bad about it, and so not want to repeat the crime. On the other hand, it is not so hard to understand their resentment, that they might want some pay-back, and that they might think it their turn to have "a place in the sun."

As with Zimbardo's experiment, things also went beyond what might be captured by a story about the reasonable claims of self-interest, or what one might reasonably expect to issue from resentment about mistreatment. So, for example, some expressed and acted upon desires to be better than, superior to, and to have power over others, and "justifications," such as that one's victims are inferior, and deserve to be treated as such, are, of course, often simply "bullshit," a "spin" to provide cover for one's appalling attitudes and motives. Just as well, such justifications commonly come to be believed, and in so doing, enable moral fog about the way we treat one another and favor ourselves.[38]

4.3.2 The Need for Intimacy

Consider another widely-shared feature of our nature crucial to shaping moral understanding and conduct – our needs for intimate connections with others. These needs spawn various fundamental values to do with love and friendship. And there is some compelling evidence, and many psychologists believe, that meeting such needs is fundamental to our wellbeing.[39] There are many ways, however, in which these needs lead us astray by blinding us to the true nature of our connections. And just as well there are many ways in which our vulnerabilities to be blinded by such needs are exploited by others. The explosion of our pursuit of social connections online presents spectacular and varied examples.

Many online scams, enabled by some of the features of online environments we set out in Chapter 2 – such as virtuality, relative anonymity and unprecedented access to one another, have targeted people's

---

[38] Often also, of course (though not in this "one off" experiment) victims can come to think they deserve it. For the film of Elliott's exercise, with an introduction and excellent concluding presentation of points by Zimbardo, along with a "reunion" video of the students with Elliott 15 years later, see, http://www.janeelliott.com/ (accessed 21 November 2017)

[39] On Maslow's hierarchy of needs they would come after physical safety and security, and so, e.g., after needs for food and shelter, but are still fundamental to wellbeing. See, A. H. Maslow: "A Theory of Human Motivation," *Psychological Review*, 50, no. 4, pp. 370–396, 1943; A. H. Maslow, *Motivation and Personality*, New York: Harper, 1954. Intimate connections seem especially important for children. See, for example: https://www.psychologytoday.com/blog/the-athletes-way/201310/ (accessed 21 November 2017); www.livescience.com/18196-maternal-support-child-brain.html (accessed 21 November 2017). And many studies seem to show that isolation and loneliness for adults present significant threats, including physical, to wellbeing. See, for example, https://www.sciencedaily.com/releases/2015/03/150311160521.htm (accessed 21 November 2017).

needs for romantic, and more generally caring and loving, connection. The television series *Catfish* presents many cases where our need for intimate connections is enabled online in ways that both blind us to the realities of what we have become, and become invested in, and make us especially vulnerable to deception and exploitation by others.

Of course, being blinded by needs of intimacy and being deceived and exploited by others is nothing new. However, features of online social worlds, and the use of such features, have especially targeted, exploited and sent astray our needs for social connection and intimacy. As we argued in Chapter 3, the drivers of apparently heightened choice and control over self-presentation and shared activity, of apparently being able to pursue life on one's own terms, the hunger for large numbers of "friends," and, often, for more famous, important or wealthy friends, are exploited and created by features of social worlds online. As a result, needs for social connection and intimacy have been increasingly directed toward the forming of "weak ties" to one another, and away from some of the basic features of the values we attach to our needs for social connection and intimacy.

4.3.3 Keeping Up with Others

A common kind of cover or obscurity about what is really going on in our lives is enabled by social pressures. Social pressures often commit us to something of a "positional arms race" or what is more commonly called "keeping up with the Jones's." These social pressures move us to keep up with others or to position ourselves relative to others to a comparable level – just as the proliferation of nuclear arms across states puts pressure on each to position themselves favorably relative to other states.

In various ways, social pressures to keep up with others, to put ourselves in a reasonable position relative to others, can lead us astray. Our social acceptance, as we suggested earlier, can often depend upon such positioning, and drive us in certain directions quite irrespective of the value of those directions. Consider a fairly mundane example – teeth whitening. Teeth whitening and better ways to do it have become major features of much of the developed world's dental health system. This puts pressure both on individuals and dental services throughout these communities to accord with the fashion. As the trend to have cosmetically enhanced white teeth takes off, my teeth look comparatively bad in a world where this is increasingly marginal and looked down upon. So irrespective of the fact that my teeth might be perfectly healthy, I am now under a lot more pressure to have whitened teeth.

As the trend takes off, dental services are increasingly under financial pressure to direct their resources this way, otherwise their business will dwindle or they will be put out of the game altogether. Both the community and the professional service industry involved now have significant imperatives to position themselves as the trend directs them. Individuals in the community have the imperative of avoiding social exclusion; the industry and its profession have the imperative of avoiding business and professional service exclusion. These imperatives have precious little to do with, and redirect resources and community interest away from, what matters about our teeth, and why we have a profession to attend to them – namely, to maintain their good health.

Following such trends avidly, therefore, can blind us to other important things. We can get caught up in such demands as wanting to avoid social and/or economic exclusion (again, without monumental unthinkingness), which nevertheless undermine and pervert our understanding of what is really going on.[40] In Chapter 3,

[40] One way in which these issues have been addressed in social science has been in terms of "conformity effects." Needs to conform to a group consensus (and so avoid, for example, social exclusion and ridicule) have been claimed to send astray, or put aside, even very simple perceptual judgments of facts, such as judging whether one line is longer than another on a piece of paper. A pioneer of this work was Solomon Asch and his "conformity experiments." See, for example, S. E. Asch, "Effects of group pressure upon the modification and distortion of judgment," in H. Guetzkow (ed.) *Groups, Leadership and Men*, Pittsburgh, PA: Carnegie Press, 1951. As noted earlier, Asch was the PhD supervisor of Stanley Milgram at Harvard. Plainly Asch had significant influence on the direction Milgram would take in the "obedience experiments" a decade later for which Milgram would become famous. See, https://www.verywell.com/solomon-asch-biography-2795519 (accessed 21 November 2017).

we described and analyzed the trends for absurdly large friendship groups, celebrity friends, and so on, in this way. Of course, teeth-whitening, and ridiculously large "friendship" groups that are dominated by weak ties, while perhaps social evils of sorts, hardly conjure up pictures of people who are evil, or who have evil minds. As we have described, however, many other cases where social positioning is especially powerful, such as some instances of extreme "pranks" and/or relentless online bullying, have certainly presented us with people who have become evil.

4.3.4 Working and Professional Life

The milieu and pressures of our working or professional lives are also a rich source of examples where a moral fog of positive and relatively neutral self-understandings operate to blind us or screen off other undesirable realities of our lives. Often, for instance, usually later in life and on reflection, professionals have felt regret about aspects of their lives that they had neglected or lost, such as their family life. Often, also, they have come to feel shame about who they have become, and how they felt emboldened to behave badly toward others through the legitimacy of their "wonderful" careers.[41]

---

[41] See, for example: Seymour Wishman, *Confessions of a Criminal Lawyer: A Memoir*, New York: N.Y, Times Books, 1981. See also the case of John Marsden, defense lawyer for serial killer Ivan Milat, who said he felt haunted at how he was able to get Milat off rape charges in the 1970s before Milat went on his killing spree. Marsden played on the fact that the two victims were lesbians in order to elicit prejudice in the jury, and somehow suggest that this would undermine the likelihood that they would be raped. Marsden won the case and within the next five years Milat went on to rape and murder a number of people. In a further twist, Marsden, it turns out, was gay and living mostly "in the closet" at that time. For some reports on the story see: Deborah Cornwall, *The 7.30 Report*, (Sydney, Australia: ABC TV), 19 July 2005, http://www.abc.net.au/7.30/content/2005/s1417948.htm (accessed 24 November 2017), and: John Marsden, "I was sacked by a serial killer," *The Sydney Morning Herald*, 4 September 2004.

The issue of how the demands or the narrow focus of our working lives can lead us to go blind to other, often more important, things is nowadays a very common theme of discussions about ethics and the workplace. One overworked staple of seminars and workshops on the subject are versions of the "invisible gorilla" videos. The audience is asked to watch a video of some people on an indoor basketball court bounce a basket-ball to one another. The audience is asked to focus on counting how many times the ball is bounced. Most manage to get the count of the bouncing ball right. In focusing on doing so however, many fail to notice a guy in a gorilla suit walk through the scene. Their narrow focus on their task blinds them to the proverbial "elephant in the room."

One way to understand how this blindness is generated is to regard it as a trick of perception. A trick such as magicians or confidence artists might use, where our attention is directed toward some distraction and so we don't see what is really going on. However, there is more going on in these workplace examples than a simple trick of perception. Having a valuable and valued working and professional identity is central to many people. And, of course, it enables many other things most of us value, such as supporting our families. Moreover, it brings with it a lifestyle of many irresistible demands, such as mortgage payments, working long hours, travelling a lot and having seemingly innumerable business meetings and dinners. Many of us have a lot invested in our working and professional life. It is the narrowing of our focus to pursuing the value of such lives, and to meeting the demands of this pursuit, that explains how our (broader) moral understanding can be blindsided when we perform our work and professional roles.

This investment in the focus of our working/professional lives – its legitimacy and value, its common and notable identity-affecting nature, and its various demands – and how all of this can also lead us astray, helps in the interpretation of another widely discussed social science experiment. In this case the subjects were seminary students at Princeton University. One group was asked to give a presentation on the tale of the "Good Samaritan." However, along the path where each subject would walk to give their presentation, an actor had been set up to play a victim of a bashing. Some of these subjects were told soon before their presentation that they were needed urgently and so needed to get a move on. Of those that thought they had to hurry, a surprising number gave cursory or nil assistance to the person in need of help. Being in a hurry to give their presentation – which was on the virtue of helping people – seemed to disable the ability of many to help someone. More than half of the theology students immersed in the subject of the ethics of assistance, aid and neighborly love made minimal, ineffective efforts.[42] So how might one resurrect the idea that having good moral character, let alone moral character that leads one to devote one's life to the ethics of assistance, is important to right and good conduct?

Of course, the force of situational factors such as "being in a hurry" when you are presented with the demand to provide some serious aid, seems, in isolation, altogether random or trivial. At the least, for anyone of moral character (much less a trainee priest), it hardly seems a compelling excuse or reason to not provide aid to someone in need. On the other hand, training to become a priest is widely thought a very worthwhile, important pursuit, and it is not hard to imagine the identity-affecting importance and demands that attach to being a trainee priest at a seminary college in Princeton. So, at the least, it is not hard to imagine that one's good judgment might become confused and conflicted. These trainee priests were not *simply* "in a hurry" but were guided by legitimate authority figures and settings to be "in a hurry," and were also in a position of learning in which they were especially dependent upon the guidance of their superiors, colleagues and settings. Given the identity-affecting importance and demands of working/professional life, and given also that in this case we are talking about students, particularly impressionable to the "letter" of such demands, it is not (as) hard to understand how their moral judg-

[42] John M. Darley and Daniel C. Batson, "'From Jerusalem to Jericho': A study of situational and dispositional variables in helping behavior," *Journal of Personality and Social Psychology*, 27, no. 1, July 1973, pp. 100–108.

ment might be led astray. If we accept that good moral character can be dependent upon such things, then such errors can be explained in terms of the moral fog that can be created when such things go wrong.[43]

4.3.5 Plural Identities

Another way in which evildoing is enabled by moral fog in our lives, is given life by the fact that our self-expressions, interactions and ways of relating to one another, as we discussed in Chapter 3, are both *plural* and *multilayered*. While these plural modes of relating enable important aspects of our basic values, they also provide worlds where the unremarkable, the good and the very bad can cohabit. And this cohabitation often generates a moral fog concerning the very bad that we do.

Jean Hatzfeld's interviews with some of those engaged in the daily murder sprees of Rwanda, is, in part, a story of plural identity, and of how this not only allows coexistence between good and evil, but of

---

[43] Many claim a strong case can be made against the very idea of moral character due to the force of situational factors in affecting right and good conduct. See, for example: Gilbert Harman, "Moral Philosophy Meets Social Psychology: Virtue Ethics and the Fundamental Attribution Error," *Proceedings of the Aristotelian Society*, New Series, 99, 1999, pp. 315–331; John Doris, *Lack of Character: Personality and Moral Behavior*, Cambridge: Cambridge University Press, 2002; John Campbell, "Can Philosophical Accounts of Altruism Accommodate Experimental Data on Helping Behavior?" *Australasian Journal of Philosophy*, 77, 1999, pp. 26–45; Mark Alfano, *Character as Moral Fiction*, Cambridge: Cambridge University Press, 2013. For those defending moral character, see, for example: Luke Russell, "Is Situationism all Bad News?" *Utilitas*, 21, no. 4, December 2009, pp. 443–463; Daniel Russell, "Aristotelian Virtue Theory: After the Person–Situation Debate," *Revue Internationale De Philosophie*, 68, no. 1, 2014; Robert M. Adams, *A Theory of Virtue: Excellence in Being for the Good*, Oxford: Clarendon Press, 2006. We discuss the attack on moral character in Chapter 5, and briefly contrast our approach to some recent efforts to defend moral character.

how this cohabitation creates a moral fog that enables the evil. Another more familiar example is given by the common depiction of gangsters or ruthless businessmen. While the ruthless businessman may be brutal to competitors or their own employees, they also may be generous, they may be loyal friends, love their children or even be great philanthropists. All of this easily works to cloud both their, and our, understanding of their brutality. As mentioned in Chapter 3, the cover of civility, and the multilayered nature of our self-expression and interaction, also provide a wellspring for obfuscation that enables evildoing – hence, the masterpiece of *Dangerous Liaisons*.

4.3.6 Incremental and Collective Evils

Some familiar forms of individual moral corruption, including "old-fashioned" evils like drinking and gambling, typically take time to develop. A "bit of a flutter" at the track or an occasional intoxicating libation is not necessarily a problem. But if they are increasingly indulged to excess, then over time there almost certainly will be some personal cost and perhaps disaster. In the meantime, however, things may not be so unbalanced. The "fall" takes time. The evils typically associated, say, with drug abuse, such as the corruption of a person's character, and their relationships with others, usually happens incrementally. In the meantime, the support of one's otherwise relatively functional life and legitimate surrounds provides some balance and some cover to blind oneself, and others, to the realities of the direction in which one is headed.[44]

In addition to evil accumulating incrementally for an individual, it may also accumulate collectively. Kernohan, building upon Joel Feinberg's notion of cumulative harm, has described how hostile

[44] On how we can descend in to evildoing in a piece-meal way, and for many historical examples and further discussion of the stories we tell ourselves about our evildoing, see, Jonathan Glover, *Humanity: A Moral History of the Twentieth Century*, 2nd Edition, New Haven, CT: Yale University Press, 2012. Thanks to Justin Oakley for referring us to Glover in this context.

environments may negatively affect a person's self-esteem and self-worth, and eventually perhaps corrode any positive sense of self altogether.[45] One slightly degrading remark may not yet be a real problem. It may be forgotten or put in context or otherwise played down. But the accumulation of many humiliating or discriminating remarks from a collective, such as many cases of online bullying attest, may do enormous damage and bring about a far more oppressive culture or atmosphere. And since the evil comes about collectively, it may easily be obscured from the viewpoint of individual perpetrators, whose remarks in themselves, need not be so terrible.

We opened our first chapter with a quote from Iris Murdoch describing evildoers as in a "swooning relationship to time." Incremental harms that accumulate over time can illustrate a "swooning" relationship, such as, for instance, immersion in the everyday activities of life, which in itself, in moderation, is not so bad, but which may lead to loss of sight of where one is headed, and of responsibility for one's conduct and oneself over time. Often, collective evils may be seen to illustrate a different kind of "swooning" relationship involved in the production of evil – namely, between individuals and a collective. Here, focus upon one's conduct as an individual, considered in isolation, need not be so bad (even over time), but it may obscure from view the collective evil that one is some part of, and hence also one's responsibility for it. Thus, for instance, the individual bully whose remarks are not so extreme, may significantly underestimate the wrongdoing involved, and his responsibility for it, by viewing his remarks in isolation, rather than viewing them in the context of being part of a collective of such remarks which are cumulatively devastating. It is clear, as many shame and blame campaigns have also illustrated, that the online world is an ideal repository where harmful content can accumulate collectively (but with little insight from individual perpetrators) to form toxic and hazardous socio-cultural environments.

---

[45] Andrew Kernohan, "Rights Against Polluters," *Environmental Ethics*, Volume 17, Issue 3, Fall, 1995, pp. 245–257; Joel Feinberg, *The Moral Limits of the Criminal Law*, Vol. 1, *Harm to Others*, Oxford, Oxford University Press, 1984, pp. 225–232.

4.3.7 Widely Shared Vice and Weakness

Most of us share various vices and weaknesses of some kind and degree. One widespread vice is self-idolatry, often referred to as narcissism.[46] It might be our power, status, achievements or our "good looks" we come to idolize. In any case, we can get lost in such images and seriously lose a grip on appropriate understanding of ourselves and others. Self-idolatry, or over-identifying with certain positive images of oneself, is also not only confined to powerful political or business leaders, movie stars, and so forth. As mentioned in Chapter 3, local heroes, such as teenage football stars, or relatively well-off professionals in their local community, such as dentists, real estate agents or accountants, commonly experience much the same problems of over-identifying with certain positive images of themselves, and with favorable comparative-competitive assessments of how they stand

[46] Narcissus, was a beautiful young man who spurned those who fell in love with his beauty. In Ovid's version the primary victim was Echo. In her despair she remained in the woods, with only the echo of her voice left to be heard. Nemesis, the goddess of revenge, decided to give Narcissus some pay-back. The revenge was for Narcissus to experience falling in love with his beauty only to experience that this love could not be reciprocated. Narcissus came upon the reflection of himself in a pond and fell in love with it. He was somewhat transfixed by his beauty, but overwhelmed by the increasing recognition that this image could not reciprocate his love for it. As a result, he fell in to the pond and drowned, or killed himself. Interestingly, the tale is a little different to some common understandings, and uses of it, in terms of self-love. According to some accounts of the tale Narcissus did not realize that the reflection he fell in love with was his own. If so, the key thing then is the falling in love with images (here an image of beauty), rather than idolizing, or falling in love with, images, because they are images of oneself. In any case, the main points of the tale seem to be about being cruel or indifferent to those who fall in love with you, or your image of beauty, and the problem of falling in love with images, i.e., images can't reciprocate your love for them. Ovid's tale appears in his *Metamorphoses*, Book iii.

relative to others.[47] As actor Jack Nicholson once observed, "Everyone has a problem with celebrity."[48]

The problem of celebrity is, in most cases, given traction by the collusion of others. Others reinforce your exalted status, such as being a wealthy dentist, or having a well-known face on television. In so doing, your self-love, in terms of such self-images, gets some independent credibility – it is not just your own fantasy to be caught up in such images.[49] If Nicholson is right, and everyone does have a problem with celebrity, then, with the support and collusion of others made possible by our online-transformed worlds, we have all now got a much bigger problem.[50] Showcasing and celebrating self-crafted

---

[47] On worries about comparative–competitive assessments, in particular, being driven to position oneself above, or as better than others, in making such assessments, see, Jeanine Grenberg's critical discussion of Aristotle's conception of the magnanimous man, in *The Ethics of Humility – A Story of Dependence, Corruption, and Virtue*, Cambridge: Cambridge University Press, 2005. For Kant this drive to make comparative–competitive assessments is part and parcel of our self-conceit. For a recent discussion of Kantian self-conceit, see Kate Moran, "Delusions of Virtue: Kant on Self-Conceit," *Kantian Review*, 19, no. 03, November 2014, pp. 419–447.

[48] American actor, born 1937.

[49] In an interesting interview, actor and director Clint Eastwood talked about his early days of fame in the United States, and some of his time in Italy in the 1960s when he starred in some excellent films of the "spaghetti western" genre. Unlike in America he could, for example, go in to a bar in Italy and not attract much attention. He relayed having the experience of being able to observe others, in their natural habitat so to speak, in contrast to being the center of their attention, and so only seeing himself, or his celebrity self, in their eyes and conduct. His point was primarily about the importance for an actor to be able to draw from observations of others. But it also highlights the different, more general, problem, for the shared life with others, of one's interaction with them being dominated by seeing images, even very positive images, of oneself in their eyes. The character of others and one's ability to observe, much less respond to them in various ways, is radically marginalized from one's interaction and shared life with them. See, Andrew Denton, *Enough Rope*, ABC Television, Australia, 24 November 2008.

[50] As we mentioned in Chapter 1, there is also some evidence from social science claiming high correlations between online use and narcissistic types.

images of oneself, being able to engage with others through such images, and being able to largely, perhaps exclusively, live in these worlds, has been a novel temptation and an opportunity taken up by many millions worldwide through some of the most popular Internet forums, such as Facebook and Instagram.[51] Such ways of expressing oneself, and forming like-minded "supportive" communities with others, have become core business online.

Evil, in a variety of ways, is close to our ordinary prosocial lives. And a common denominator for how evil is enabled to be so close, are the variety of ways in which features of our ordinary, prosocial lives can bring about moral fog. Our understanding of the minds of evildoers, and varieties of moral fog, has been guided by thinking about how moral character and the moral life are shaped across the related fronts of issues concerning our nature, our shared lives and our environment. In particular, we have highlighted some of the important interests, needs, demands and limitations in relation to the development and maintenance of moral character across these fronts, and how they shape our lives for better or worse. In so doing, we have seen how evil can be close by our otherwise relatively prosocial lives in a very fundamental way. Many of the features that make the prosocial, moral life possible, such as our dependence upon the support and direction of others, can also undermine it.[52]

---

[51] Of course, such online sites and forums are not just about this. But it is hard to ignore how dominant and widespread these expressions of self and ways of relating to others have become online.

[52] Our metaphysical and epistemological view of the moral life involves significant and unavoidable complexity, uncertainty, limits and risks, including limits regarding individual moral imagination and understanding, and our dependence upon others on both counts. Other views, such as the tragic view mentioned in our preface, have a similar outlook. While we think these features of the moral life are significant, unavoidable and have a much bigger place in our lives than many of us like to think, we are not so fatalistic about the obstacles they present. Highlighting and better understanding the problems for normative competence presented by the moral fog of our worlds ought to (and might even actually) help better address such problems and so develop better ways to navigate and design our worlds.

5

The Fate of the Moral Life

"When we survey our lives and endeavors, we soon observe that almost the whole of our actions and desires is bound up with the existence of other human beings. We notice that our whole nature resembles that of the social animals. We eat food that others have produced, wear clothes that others have made, live in houses that others have built. The greater part of our knowledge and beliefs has been communicated to us by other people through the medium of a language which others have created. Without language our mental capacities would be poor indeed, comparable to those of the higher animals; we have, therefore, to admit that we owe our principal advantage over the beasts to the fact of living in human society. The individual, if left alone from birth, would remain primitive and beastlike in his thoughts and feelings to a degree that we can hardly conceive."

Albert Einstein[1]

[1] Yes…Albert Einstein, Physicist, 1879–1955. It is, of course, often a mistake to take as instructive or interesting what a genius, say, in physics or music, might say about philosophical questions. Whether true in this case or not, the quote is far too apt for our purposes to resist. (Along, of course, with the fact that it is Einstein.) Aristotle is a little more widely known (in philosophical circles) for highlighting various ways in which good moral character is dependent upon the external goods provided by the world and others. In Chapter 3 we presented Aristotle's argument that we need friends for self-knowledge, and we need self-knowledge for virtue, and so we cannot be self-sufficient in virtue. See also, e.g., *Nicomachean Ethics*: "[Happiness/*Eudaimonia*] needs the external goods as well, for it is impossible, or not easy, to do noble acts without the proper equipment…" Book I, 8, 1099b32–4; The discussion at the end of Book I, 9, of the misfortunes of Priam; Book I,10, throughout; "Hence we ought to have been brought up in a particular way from our very youth, as Plato says, so as both to delight in

Evil Online, First Edition. Dean Cocking and Jeroen van den Hoven.

5.1 Introduction

The shared life, or ideals thereof, have long been thought to provide the grounds upon which virtuous character and the good life are created and sustained. Aristotle presented friendship as his central example of how the shared life provides a fundamental model of the good life.[2] We have suggested, especially in Chapter 3, various ways in which the nature of our shared lives enables our values. Mostly, however, we have focused on how the shared life just as effectively creates and sustains evil. Indeed, we have just argued that evil is often close by the prosocial life in a very fundamental way. Many features that make such a life possible also enable its downfall.

5.2 Moral Character: A Case of Mistaken Identity?

Some influential approaches to evildoing, and relations between moral character, others and surrounds, from both philosophy and more recent social science, have not seen things this way. Instead, *good* moral character has been thought of as much more independent from, and resistant to, self-interest and the influence of others and surrounds. The basic idea is that if self-interest, and the demands or permissions of others and/or circumstances, would lead you to act wrongly, then, as a responsible adult of good moral character, you would reject such direction. However, as a result of worries about whether good moral character is really like this – i.e., generally able to be independent from, and resilient against, such influences – the very notion of moral character has come under significant question and attack.

---

and be pained by the things that we ought; this is the right education," Book II, 3, 1104b11–13, and; "A certain training in virtue arises also from the company of the good, as Theognis has said before us," Book IX, 9, 1170a10–11. Thanks to Justin Oakley for these latter references.

[2] See, Aristotle, *Nichomachean Ethics*, *op. cit.*, especially books VIII and IV. See also, the previous note.

A foundational presentation from philosophy that supposes this view of good moral character – whereby it stands independent of, and resilient against, temptations to act wrongly – but then leads us to question it, comes from Plato's tale of the Ring of Gyges.[3] The tale is the classic illustration of the worry – presented by conditions where one "can get away with" antisocial or immoral conduct – that good moral character might be something of a fiction. We are asked to imagine that we have a ring that makes us invisible. Invisibility, and so anonymity, means we could act in antisocial and immoral ways with impunity. We need not be accountable to the laws, conventions and reactions of others since we can avoid their enforcement. For Plato, and many philosophy classes since, the tale leads us to ask: What reasons are left to be moral? Is the wellspring for moral conduct and character really just self-interest?

If it is *just* the unavoidable accountability to others that is doing the work (in the sense of regulating one's conduct toward others in line with the fact that one cannot avoid their punishment or censure and so get away with treating them badly), then prosocial, moral attitudes and conduct seem to reduce to self-interest. In seemingly sufficiently socially and morally functional worlds, it turns out that we conduct ourselves in generally civil and morally responsive ways toward one another, not because we "really" have such attitudes and motives, but because it would be against our self-interest to behave otherwise. So is this what the flourishing of evil, or otherwise, really comes to? Is "good moral character" a real thing, or do attributions of good moral character really just turn out to be a case of mistaken identity?

On the back of experiments in social psychology, many have argued that since our so-called prosocial and moral sensibilities seem so easily overturned by settings permitting or enabling evil, that the very idea of moral character is a fiction or, at least, largely misguided. The flourishing of good and evil is (mostly) about the settings we are placed in. In a balanced presentation of this approach, Zimbardo says:

---

[3] Plato, *The Republic*, Book 11, 359b–360b, Penguin Classics, Penguin Books (Publisher), 1974.

The Lucifer Effect raises a fundamental question about the nature of human nature: How is it possible for ordinary, average, even good people to become perpetrators of evil? In trying to understand unusual, or aberrant behavior, we often err in focusing exclusively on the inner determinants of genes, personality, and character, as we also tend to ignore what may be the critical catalyst for behavior change in the external Situation or in the System that creates and maintains such situations. I challenge readers to reflect on how well they really know themselves, and how much confidence they have in what they would or would not ever do when put into new behavioral settings."[4]

---

[4] "Overview," *op. cit.* Some writers have rejected these sorts of challenges or worries for moral character, by rejecting their assumption or claim that we can take our lessons about moral character by looking at how people behave under fairly extreme and aberrant conditions. So, for example R. M. Adams says: "in thinking about the moral excellences and deficiencies that people who will never experience anything like Auschwitz, there is little moral illumination to be gained by speculating about how they would have responded to an extremely malignant environment of that sort." – R. M. Adams, *A Theory of Virtue: Excellence in Being for the Good*, *op. cit.*, p. 161. And about *Lord Jim*, John Doris says, "The misproportion is that Jim reached a conclusion about himself more global than a single behavior warrants; despite the *Patna* debacle, there was much about Jim "worth having"" – John Doris, *Lack of Character: Personality and Moral Behavior*, *op. cit.*, 2002, pp. 160–164. We thank Justin Oakley for both quotes, and he makes the following points: first, (to sum up the above) failing to act well in a "perfect storm" (for failing to act well) need not impugn claims that one would act well under conditions that were not so extreme, and second, a person can be "too hard" on themselves – so Zimbardo's worry also goes the other way, i.e., how confident are you about how *others* would behave under such conditions. We agree with these points. The account we have developed of moral character in the face of its failure under various conditions, and our account of much of this failure in terms of the moral fog of evildoing, hopefully adds quite a bit more to such approaches to the defense of moral character. Thus, for instance, many of our cases of evil online, such as online bullying and shaming, are hardly at the aberrant extremes of, say, Auschwitz. And our problems of moral fog apply in many cases that go beyond or have nothing to do with the problem of unjustifiably demonizing a person on account of a single behavior or incident (as, for example, we too often see in cases of online shaming, but we do not see at all, for instance, in worrying trends such as the dominance of "weak ties" online, or the demolition of our plural worlds

According to many, in focusing on moral character we have been making what has been called "the fundamental attribution error." We have become used to thinking about one another as having certain sorts of character traits, and to understanding behavior in these terms. So, for example, we attribute to someone's helping behavior that they are compassionate or empathetic, or to their harming behavior that they are vicious or cruel. Apparently, however, our long-standing focus on the notion of good or bad character as the wellspring for good or bad conduct, and so of what we should be concerned about, as parents, friends or a community, has been in error. People's behavior, it turns out, cannot be (much) explained by such appeals to character. Instead, helping or harming behaviors are to be explained (or generally and much better explained) by the external features of the environment within which we act.

But if the worry put to us by Plato's presentation of Glaucon's tale of the Ring of Gyges is right, i.e., that our reasons to be moral just collapse back to reasons of self-interest, then the lesson need not be that moral character is largely irrelevant in determining behavior. The lesson need not be that we have been in error in attributing moral character to people. On the contrary, the problem might be that, as a result of being fundamentally self-interested, we are thereby also fundamentally evil.[5] Moral behavior may be determined then, not by the impact of features of the external world upon our *lack* of moral character, but rather, the impact of such features upon our *bad* character. In particular, we require a suite of "enforcements" to make it in our self-interest to not run riot over the legitimate claims of others. Take these enforcements away, and allow us free reign, and we run amok.

---

of public and private life online, or particular cases, such as the corruption of the vulnerable brought by pro-anorexia sites). See also ahead for some more on how our approach to understanding moral character in the face of situationist challenges differs from some other recent approaches.

[5] As noted earlier, Kant thought we were radically evil in the sense that our propensity to put self-interest above the moral law is significant and ubiquitous.

Our experiments in social psychology, therefore, need not show how easily "good" people can turn bad. They need not show that moral character is not efficacious in producing conduct, or that situational forces morph us in to evil beings quite alien to our usual good nature. Instead of there being a "Lucifer effect," we may simply be letting the cat out of the bag. At best, or worst, the fundamental attribution error we have made has been to suppose that *good* moral character exists. Obviously, however, none of this helps friends of the view that good moral character is important to the flourishing of the good and resisting the bad.

5.3 Good Character, Self-interest, Others and Surrounds

We do not think people are fundamentally evil, altogether governed by self-interest, that moral character is a fiction, or that our social science experiments show that prosocial, good moral character plays little explanatory role in conduct. Instead, the understandings of good moral character that spawn these views are mistaken. So we need to do some revisionary work on these common ways to think about good moral character.

As we have suggested, good moral character has commonly been understood in terms of its independence from, its contrast to, and its resilience against, the claims of self-interest. And it has also been commonly understood in terms of its effectiveness in being able to issue in good conduct quite independently of the need of support from others and surrounds. Kant, for example, plainly invokes the latter requirement in defining immaturity of enlightenment (and so immaturity of moral character) as the inability to use one's understanding without the guidance of another.[6] (In fairly stark contrast to Aristotle's view, noted above, that it does not make sense to think we

[6] Kant, What is enlightenment? *The Berlin Monthly*, 1784.

are self-sufficient in virtue, and to Einstein's view with which we started this chapter.[7])

While, of course, Kant's point fits many cases (notably, children and young people), if we are to understand moral character in this way generally, then given the evidence from social psychology, and no doubt our everyday lives, there really does not seem much of a role for individual "enlightenment," or good moral character. At best, good character plays a small part in determining whether or not we conduct ourselves in socially and morally acceptable ways. Many experiments in social psychology and many compelling descriptions of "real life" evildoing show a failure of moral character, so understood, in the face of inclinations and circumstances, such as to position oneself well, obey authority figures, and where there is permission from those of influence, to run amok. Accordingly, if Kant (along with many others[8]) were right about the nature of good moral character, in practice it seems of little explanatory relevance to the flourishing of the good and resisting the bad.[9]

---

[7] See also, Nancy Sherman, *Making a Necessity of Virtue: Aristotle and Kant on Virtue*, Cambridge, Cambridge University Press, 1997, especially chapters 3 and 4, and on Kant, especially his Stoic influence; Justin Oakley and Dean Cocking, *Virtue Ethics and Professional Roles*, Cambridge, Cambridge University Press, 2001, especially Chapter 6, section 3.

[8] See also, of course, Plato's allegory of the cave – the classic illustration of true knowledge beyond the bounds of our experience in the actual world; *The Republic, op. cit.*, Book VII, 514a–520a.

[9] As mentioned earlier in Chapter 4, a number of writers have defended moral character in this context. So, for example, Daniel Russell highlights the need to look at how different people construe the moral demands of their situation, not simply at how they behave. This then allows us to see how, for example, two people of moral character (or one, but in different situations), may be moved by moral concern for others, but be led to behave in seemingly conflicting ways. Thus, for instance, Russell describes how our hapless priests might, when they are in a hurry, be moved by the (moral) concern to not keep their audience waiting. See, Russell, *op. cit.*, pp. 40–41. See also pp. 44–46, for some further suggestions as to how moral concern for others can be thought to remain relevant to the flourishing of the good and resisting the bad in such cases where it seems to have gone astray. One worry for this approach to understanding the good moral character of some of our priests,

However, as much of our discussion suggests, good moral character is not only about its independence from, and contrast to, the claims of self-interest. There are reasonable claims of self-interest upon moral character. We have seen, for instance, how people seek to avoid the risk of social exclusion by keeping pace with certain prevailing attitudes and trends, which nevertheless may lead them to miss what matters most and to act badly. However, we also saw how being led astray was not necessarily because people are selfish or inclined to run amok when they can. On the contrary, it was because, given the circumstances, they had *some* good reason to so behave – namely, to avoid social exclusion. "Happy hermits" aside, there are few of us who could flourish without social inclusion.

Good moral character is also not only about its efficaciousness without the need of support (or, indeed, in the face of opposition) from others and surrounds.[10] As we have seen (notably in Chapter 3),

in terms of their other-regarding concern to not keep their audiences waiting, is that it seems to leave us with a fairly ludicrous view of the concern for others that a person of good moral judgment would be guided by in the circumstances. The other-regarding demand to help a victim of a bashing plainly trumps any conflicting demand to not keep an audience waiting. Instead of this focus on other-regarding concern, and how this might be construed so as to rehabilitate the efficacy of good moral character, the focus of our approach has been to highlight other demands and vulnerabilities of good moral character. One sharp contrast we reject is between good moral character and the demands of self-interest. The other, related, sharp contrast our approach to moral character rejects, is between an internal world "of one's own" and an external world of others and surrounds. This expansion of how to understand moral character (for instance, by including the reasonable demands of self-interest, and vulnerabilities, such as our trust in the influence of those from whom we learn), clearly goes way beyond, and in very different directions to, pointing to how moral concern can (appropriately) have conflicting objects in a given case, or may be worthy of the name even though it fails occasionally, or how altruism is very rare anyway, (to list some of the main moves that have been made by defenders of moral character in this context).

[10] We do not, of course, deny that these pictures of good moral character are important, even basic. Also, of course, Kant recognized that there are reasonable claims of self-interest, and that there are moral duties to self.

our moral imagination and understanding about important aspects of our basic values, and how we create and sustain these aspects of our values, continues, in various ways, to depend upon others, and the settings of our interaction. Imagine, for instance, the *other side* of Plato's tale of the Ring of Gyges, i.e., the other side of the opportunity to run amok in a world of anonymity. Imagine that you are somehow stuck with this ring on your finger, and so now you are quite altogether excluded from the social world. Imagine further that you have intimate, loving relationships with a partner, family, and friends. They could now not see you loving them, nor you their replies, and so on. Instead of offering the opportunity to run amok, this setting of anonymity would be a wretched curse. You would now lose much of your shared life, and those aspects of yourself that go with it, in particular, the self-expression and evolving development that comes with the ongoing and dynamic interaction of your mutual loves.

We suggest then, revising two common ways in which good moral character has been understood (and so two revisions of debates about the fate of moral character given the apparent impact of situational influences). First, we reject the sharp contrast between moral reasons and reasons of self-interest, since some reasons of self-interest invoke claims that would (reasonably) impact upon, or be considered by, a person of moral character (even if these claims should not win the day). Second, we reject the sharp contrast between our "internal" and "external" worlds that is often at play in characterizations of moral character, and that dominates discussions of the efficacy of good moral character in producing right conduct. Often it is the interplay between facts about our own psychologies and facts about the external world that we need to appreciate if we are to understand the nature of moral character and the fate of our reasons and conduct. Thus, for example, we have seen how important features of our basic values and of our legitimate needs and vulnerabilities regarding our connections to others, such as in intimacy and learning, are plainly relational in kind and dependent upon facts about the external world of others and our settings.

Our judgments about the fate of good moral character in certain settings, such as settings where one is left to remain anonymous, are fundamentally influenced by how we understand good moral character. If we understand good moral character as something that is dependent for its creation and sustenance upon certain kinds of relations with others, and upon certain kinds of worlds of communication and interaction with others, then the Ring of Gyges presents a very different kind of morality tale than usually thought. Imagining that we might be corrupted and behave badly if we had a ring that made us invisible, and so were able to avoid punishment and censure, should not lead us to worry that our "moral" reasons really just collapse back to reasons of self-interest, and to worry whether there really is such a thing as good moral character. The tale should certainly lead us to worry about the fate of moral character. But the worry is not that moral character might be a fiction. Instead, the worry is how good moral character may be corrupted when the world is designed such that it takes away the kinds of relationships with others, and the kinds of settings, upon which the flourishing of good moral character depends. If we were somehow stuck with this ring, where our ability to relate to others has gone so wrong, then our good moral character and its possibilities are very vulnerable, and we may well come to make bad choices, lose ourselves, and perhaps descend altogether into evil or insanity.

The Internet and its many applications and services are design products, the end result of a long history of many design decisions. Decisions that impact upon how we pursue our lives in all sorts of ways. (Some of which may be intended, some more of which may be foreseen, and many of which are certainly unintended altogether.) What we can do, what we can be, or share, send, upload, download, on which conditions, and at what price, are all part of the architecture of the Internet and World Wide Web. The medium of our online-transformed worlds seduces and invites certain options, and constrains and rules out others. The fact, for instance, that any uploaded information about oneself thereby becomes the property of a social networking site are identity-relevant defaults, i.e., design features that shape the sort of identities we are able, or more likely, to create. The fact, for example, that there is no limit to the number of "friends" one can add to one's profile (along with various other features we canvassed in Chapter 3 about how we can present ourselves and interact with others online), imposes certain ways of thinking about intimacy and ourselves.

Another notable change brought by our online-transformed worlds concerns our learning practices. As we have indicated, one important example of how our moral condition is generated and sustained, concerns how our learning is typically very dependent upon, say, parents, teachers, mentors, colleagues and intimates, to help us navigate our way in life (especially through relatively unfamiliar territory and well beyond when we are young). Some experiments in social psychology show an illustrative extension of this general phenomenon of our reliance upon those more "expert" in unfamiliar territory to guide us in our conduct, and how this reliance can lead us astray. However, apart from the problem of being led astray by those we might unavoidably need to rely upon, the relative unfamiliarity of parents and educators with the cutting edge applications of the Web that youth and children are constantly exploring (and to whom such applications are largely targeted), means that our young people cannot really expect much guidance and assistance in navigating their way through these new social worlds. In fact, often enough, as many parents will attest, immersion online provides a "second life" for children and teenagers quite separate from parental navigation. This is in stark contrast with our traditional worlds, where we are accustomed to being able to provide the appropriate and timely parental feedback that we all have long recognized is essential to functional moral and social development.

As just mentioned, the communication environment into which the Internet has developed is significantly characterized by features that were not anticipated, much less intentionally designed. The Internet was designed to form a robust medium for sharing data and computing capacity in science and the military domain without centralized control. It was conceived as an infrastructure for connecting serious, well-intending institutional actors interested in sharing research resources. It was not designed for communication between private persons, or for fostering "personal" relationships between them. One of the distinctive features (and attractions) of online communication to which we have drawn attention is the seemingly heightened choice and control, absent of the influence of others and settings in our traditional worlds, offered by our online-transformed worlds. Now, for instance, we may have relative isolation from the social influence, engagement and various external controls that apply in our traditional worlds. Laws, regulations and social conventions often do not apply, or are difficult to apply, and the alternative replacement worlds provided online often marginalize the normalizing influence and feedback of others, such as from family, friends or work colleagues.

Against such psychosocial environments, we have argued that our values are unavoidably and desirably developed in light of various features of our nature, and of our interactions with one another, that have long been enabled and fine-tuned by the communication forums of our traditional worlds. Thus, for instance, we argued against the trend to (seemingly) live life on one's own terms, and we have highlighted ways in which some basic values are given expression in virtue of our inhabiting and navigating the plural worlds of public and private life, and how much of this is lost in the flat-lining of these worlds online.

Obviously, the moral character of our lives, for better or worse, and whether online or not, depends significantly upon our surrounding milieu – our families, friends, mentors and the suite of social, political, legal and economic institutions and conventions within which we live. And many are unfortunate in our traditional worlds. Many, for example, are brought up in dysfunctional worlds of abuse, discrimination and misery. In many ways, then, it may be better that we were nurtured elsewhere, perhaps in an online environment where, for example, the color of one's skin, one's acne or speech impediment will not "get in the way" in relations with others or provide grounds to be discriminated against.

There are many cases where the advent of the Internet has changed people's lives in very positive ways by providing such alternative and replacement social worlds. As we have mentioned, the relative anonymity the Internet offers, has, for example, widely been associated with disappearing bias, prejudices and discrimination of people on the basis of appearances, dress, accent, ethnic origin and gender typically associated with face-to-face interaction. Our claims against living in such worlds does not discount any of this. Many of the significant and distinctive features of online worlds, and our use of them, such as the information revolution, have enabled both great goods and great evils. So, too, for the social revolution that has now become the dominant use of online worlds.

A number of further queries may be put against our approach, and it will be helpful to address them so that we might better understand our problems of evil. The first objection we want to discuss concerns questions about responsibility for wrong and evildoing, and about the nature of evil. The second objection denies that our online-transformed worlds present any notable, new problems of evil. And the third objects that our approach would tear down what is so awesome about the Internet – namely, its relatively unregulated, anarchic freedom of expression and activity.

5.4 Evil and Responsibility

The term "evil" is sometimes used in philosophical discussion interchangeably with the terms "bad" or "wrong." So whatever is bad or wrong, such as lying, cheating or stealing, has also been referred to as evil. In this way, evil has been understood simply and broadly in contrast to what is good or right. As noted in our preface, Kant, for example, seems to have regarded an evil will simply and broadly in terms of failing to have a good will.[11] Common usage, however, and most philosophical discussion more directly focused on analyzing evil, has in mind things that are bad or wrong in extreme or fundamental ways. So, for example, the Holocaust, Rwanda or serial rapists and murderers – not garden-variety lying, cheating, or stealing. Thus, on this common conception, evil is characterized not only by contrast to what is good or right, but also by contrast to what is merely bad or wrong. Most of our cases are like this, though some are obviously worse than others, and some maybe wrong or bad but not in that sense.

---

[11] Immanuel Kant, Religion within the boundaries of mere reason, in *Religion and Rational Theology* Op cit.

So what makes something evil, beyond what is wrong or bad? It would take us a long way from our main focus on the moral fog of wrong and evildoing, both online and in our traditional worlds, to go too far down this track. Nevertheless, thinking of wrong and evildoing as undertaken in a moral fog might seem at odds with being able to hold the perpetrators morally responsible, and/or fall well short of what is required for regarding someone as evil, or as possessing an evil mind. Since we do think that moral responsibility can be attributed to evildoing undertaken in a moral fog, and that the picture of a "fogged up" evildoer can illustrate an evil mind or character, we need to address these queries.

It is widely agreed across discussions of moral responsibility that attributions of moral responsibility for wrong and evildoing require that the person understood (or was capable of understanding) that their conduct was wrong or evil. The fact that this requirement is not met by children or the insane (to use the standard examples) is precisely why we think they are incapable of having moral responsibility attributed to them. But, of course, plenty of sane adults have done terrible things under conditions of compromised moral understanding, where they fail to understand the wrong that they do, such as, for instance, when they are drunk (to give another standard example). Yet we nevertheless believe that they are capable of such understanding, and so, on account of this, that they can have moral responsibility attributed to them. People can be culpably ignorant of the wrong they do – namely, when we judge they were in a position prior to their compromised understanding where they could be expected to foresee the wrong that they would do (or risked doing), and they were able to avoid this coming about. Commonly then, the requirement of moral understanding for ascribing moral responsibility is in the past.[12] We cannot require moral understanding at a

[12] We focus here on the requirement that the person understands right from wrong. We do so, of course, since this is what is compromised in cases of evil undertaken in a moral fog. The requirement of moral understanding for attributions of moral responsibility for wrong and evildoing, however, is quite broad, and will have a number of requirements under it regarding other capacities, such as the capacity for instrumental reasoning concerning one's

current time, or even that a wrongdoer has any capacity for appropriate moral understanding left in them at all. After all, these things may well be true of a drunk driver, whom, nevertheless, we judge, bears, in his past, some moral responsibility for what he has become, and the wrong he now commits.

On our approach, otherwise fairly prosocial people in the grip of some kind of moral fog may commit evil. Since we are imagining people who are otherwise fairly prosocial, we are imagining people who have, at least, possessed the necessary cognitive/affective capacities for appropriate moral understanding. We are imagining people who we would normally regard as fit for attributions of moral responsibility. So the question is: how much culpability do they bear for their downfall? Looked at in this way, there is nothing especially peculiar about thinking of evildoers as in a moral fog, so far as ascribing moral responsibility goes. Whether or not someone is responsible for evil undertaken in a moral fog is a question of their culpability for being in their current state of moral fog (just as whether the ignorant evildoer is responsible for their evildoing is a question of their culpability for their current ignorance that results in their evildoing).[13]

On the other hand, if there is a problem, it is that we are arguing that morally fogged up worlds have a notable place in our lives. We do

---

beliefs and desires. On this, and some other capacities necessary for attributions of moral responsibility for wrongdoing, see Michael Smith, Beyond belief, desire and rationality, or: the unsettling truth about conditions of responsibility, in *Compatibilist Responsibility: Beyond Free Will and Determinism*, Nicole Vincent, Ibo van de Poel, Jeroen van den Hoven, (eds), New York: Springer Publishing, 2011, pp. 53–70.

[13] Whether or not this widely used tracing approach to attributing moral responsibility works is a different question. We suggest ahead that on our account of the moral fog of evildoing, satisfying the epistemic condition for attributing moral responsibility in candidate cases of culpable ignorance, may, in many instances, be especially unlikely. (Not that this need be a problem for us, or for the tracing approach.) For a good discussion of the problems and some careful defense of the tracing approach, see, Kevin Tempe, Tracing and the epistemic condition of responsibility, *The Modern Schoolman*, Department of Philosophy, Saint Louis University, 88, no. 1/2, January/April 2011, pp. 5–28.

think that these worlds can mitigate individual moral responsibility, and we think that this occurs in a range of ways, and a good deal more than we usually recognize. Thus, we think problems of moral fog not only present significant problems for moral understanding and normative competence, but in so doing can also present significant and widespread forms of injustice, both for individuals and communities, concerning the meaning people are able to give their lives.[14]

Zimbardo challenged us to reflect upon how well we all might act under certain conditions. Our story aims to help better understand the vulnerability of the moral life, in particular, the vulnerability of our capacities for moral understanding, due to the impact of others and features of our surrounds. Our capacities for moral understanding, what we can imagine, or how we apply it in practice, is very much enabled, or undermined, by our socialization. Many point to the need for more individual reasoning, reflection and moral imagination if we are to dig our way out of the moral abyss our settings might otherwise leave us in. However, whilst a necessary and important part of the moral life, there are limits to what we can come up with ourselves. What we can imagine, our capacities for moral reflection, and our abilities to apply these appropriately in practice, are also, in various ways and to some degree, in the hands of the world around us.

Consider, for example, how the influence of others and our settings also commonly enables and sustains in us appropriate, and often far more expansive and richer, moral understandings that go way beyond anything we might come up with ourselves.[15] This was an important

[14] Namely, in cases where the failure of moral understanding was (in some notable part) due to the inordinate and hard to avoid undermining influence of the design of one's settings and/or others.

[15] For a classic tale of this terrain see Frank Capra's masterpiece, *It's a Wonderful Life*, Liberty Films (Producers), 1946. The film is a fountain of evocative, fairly ordinary or commonplace, and often quite funny, illustrations. It also, of course, (by showing George Bailey, played by James Stewart, what the world would have been like without him) highlights how, just as we may be shaped by our world far more than we often recognize, so too we

part of the story we told in Chapter 3, regarding the plurality and relational nature of our values, and the kinds of settings of self-expression and communication we require if we are to achieve them. In virtue of our inhabiting worlds with others where plural forms of self-expression and communication flourish, important relational aspects of our values are enabled and sustained, including such values as autonomy and privacy that are concerned with how we might best promote individual self-governance and control.

In the case of the social revolution online technology has delivered, meeting the epistemic requirement for moral understanding necessary for attributions of culpable ignorance, i.e., that I know (or it is reasonable to expect that I foresee the unacceptable risk) that my choices will lead me a certain way down the track, is especially problematic. The interpretive flexibility of the revolutionary medium, for instance, throws up significant uncertainty of its own about how to understand the moral terrain. In particular, this feature, common across technological advance, can radically fog up our predictive abilities as to where our conduct might lead us, well beyond the usual conditions of complexity and uncertainty faced by our efforts to understand what we are doing. Thinking of evildoing as undertaken in a moral fog does not rule out ascribing moral responsibility, and we certainly would not want it to do so necessarily.[16] However, varieties of moral fog do illustrate ways in which our moral responsibility, like our personhood generally, is much more in the hands of others and our settings than most of us normally think. And if we are on the right track, then online technology has brought significant additional and distinctive problems of its own across these fronts.

---

shape the world far more than we often recognize. See also the sensational Australian film, *The Sum of Us*, The Australian Film Finance Commission, Great Sum Film Limited Partnership, Samuel Goldwyn Company, The Southern Star Entertainment (Producers), 1994.

[16] As, for example, Tempe says: "Merely not thinking about the moral status of one's actions ought not undermine one's moral responsibilities for those actions." *op. cit.*, p. 19.

Let us turn then to the query of why we should regard the "fogged up" mind (much less the person) as evil. Writers concerned to characterize the nature of evil (as against garden-variety wrong-doing) often appeal to sadistic desires or feelings in characterizing evil agency, and what they have in mind are desires or feelings that are grounded upon and guided by an understanding that one's conduct will cause significant harm. Without this understanding, i.e., that you would cause significant harm by doing a certain thing, then citing sadistic desires or feelings to do that thing could not explain its being done. The requirement of moral understanding is assumed by the characterization of evil agency in terms of sadistic desire.[17]

[17] At the same time it seems to render the sadistic desire irrational or insane. After all, it claims you understand that the harm is evil. But if you understand that it is evil, then you understand that it is at the far end of what you have reason to choose. Yet you do so. But how can this even count as a choice? If, for example, I recognize that it is against all reason to wear a blindfold when I drive my car, then how do we make sense of the suggestion that I would *choose* to do so? I am "choosing" to do, what, by my own lights, I recognize I have most reason *not* to do. It seems then, that I am just utterly out of control. But perhaps the sadist does not really think the harm they cause is (overall) evil. They may, for example, think the harm is bad but that pursuing their own pleasure from inflicting the harm is a more compelling good, and so permissible or right. (Recall, for example, Morton's suggestion that the evil-doer's attraction to evil might not be the evil itself – and so very difficult to understand – but some positive images of evildoers, such as can be found in novels or films.) If so, since the evildoer's moral understanding is so off the wall (mistaken), we again face the problem that their conduct seems irrational or insane. Even if, for example, we could tell a story of their upbringing that made some sense of how they came to have (and were unable to shake) such shockingly mistaken moral beliefs, they still have shockingly mistaken moral beliefs. They still fall monumentally short in their capacities for moral understanding. For some discussion of issues that arise where forms of rationality or sanity are the key requirements for ascribing moral responsibility, including how ascribing moral responsibility may then be ruled out for those whose beliefs about the evil they do are mistaken, see Michael Smith, *op. cit.*, and Susan Wolf, Sanity and the metaphysics of responsibility, in *Responsibility, Character and the Emotions: New Essays in Moral Psychology* (Ferdinand

Similarly, in defining evil action, Todd Calder says: "The essential properties of evil actions include a victim's significant harm and a perpetrators e-motivation. An e-motivation consists in an inexcusable intention to bring about, allow, or witness, significant harm for an unworthy goal."[18] But you cannot *intend* to bring about, allow, or witness, significant harm if you do not understand what you are doing under that description. Of course, it may be true that you should have understood, and that you are responsible for this failure of understanding, and for the harm involved in the conduct that you do intend. But if you do not understand that harm is involved, then the harm that is involved cannot be one of the things that you intend. So while Calder's definition opens up more faces of evil than those who focus too much on just one picture of evil, such as presented by the sadist, his account of evil motivations does share the requirement (of evil agency) that the evildoer must understand their conduct as causing significant harm, and so evil.[19] This requirement of moral

Schoeman, ed.), Cambridge, Cambridge University Press, 1987 pp. 46–62, pp. 61–62. See also, our brief discussion in Chapter 4.

[18] Todd Calder, Is evil just very wrong? *Philosophical Studies*, 163, 2013, pp. 177–196, p. 194.

[19] In a more expansive and nuanced definition, Calder says: "I call combinations of desires for other people's significant harm or for objects or states of affairs inconsistent with other people's being spared serious harm, together with the lack of a desire that they not be significantly harmed, e-desire sets. I contend that e-desire sets are constitutive of the motivation necessary for evil." Todd Calder, *The apparent banality of evil, op. cit.*, p. 366. Here, Calder may capture one kind of evildoer who fails to understand the evil they do, as nevertheless being of an evil mind. He may capture the evildoer who (in any case) lacks the desire that other people not be significantly harmed by their conduct. If lacking the desire to avoid harming others is taken to mean that the evildoer would nevertheless have gone ahead with their evildoing – even when they did understand and foresee the harm they would cause – then you might think this suffices to describe them as being of an evil mind. Thus, since they would have gone ahead with their evildoing anyway, they do not get off the hook (of having an evil mind) on account of their not understanding the evil they were doing in the actual case. This, however, would not capture many of our cases of evildoing undertaken in a moral fog. As we have highlighted throughout, the moral fog of evildoing describes and explains

understanding then, is widely-held across otherwise quite different views about what constitutes an evil mind.[20]

So why think of our "fogged up" mind, where the person does not really understand that their conduct is evil, and so need not desire that they bring about evil, as an evil mind? At the least, surely such a mind is well short of the evilness of those who are directly guided by the desire to bring about evil by their recognition that it is evil? (Such as we might imagine with the sadist.) Indeed, surely it is well short of the evilness of the minds of those who, while not aiming at the evil they cause, understand and so foresee that their conduct is evil, but nevertheless go ahead in pursuit of their own perceived self-interest? (As we see, for instance, in many cases of murder for financial gain, and would also fit Kant's view of evil as undertaken from self-conceit.)[21]

---

many cases of evildoing undertaken by those of otherwise fairly prosocial minds – people who do have the desire to avoid harming others.

[20] Claudia Card's account of evil is an exception. Card's account tells us that evils are reasonably foreseen intolerable harms produced by inexcusable wrong-doing. See, Claudia Card, *The Atrocity Paradigm: A Theory of Evil*, New York: Oxford University Press, 2002, p. 16. Card's focus was on the intolerable harm suffered by victims, rather than on the motives of the evildoer. Her inclusion of the mind of the evildoer requires only that they are morally culpable for evil in that: the significant harm was reasonably foreseeable (whether the agent did foresee the harm or not); that there was no justification (and so the harm was evil), and; that there was no excuse undermining responsibility for the harm. Her account, therefore, allows a much broader view of the sort of minds that may qualify for evil, and does not require attitudes that are understanding of, or desire sets that are guided by, the evil involved. Thus, her view could count a banal mind, or a morally fogged up mind, as evil.

[21] The propensity to favor self-interest over the moral law need not at all involve being moved by desires to bring about evil (either directly or indirectly). As we noted in Chapter 4, Kant, contrary to Aristotle, regarded evil as common across our nature, rather than bestial in the sense of beyond human vice and weakness. In this way then, Kant may (again) have been something of a trailblazer in the move away from thinking of evildoers as guided by evil, and toward thinking of evildoers as well within the frame of ordinary human vice and weakness. Harry Lime (another famous character played – and

Arendt, and her supporters, have long argued that the evilness of the banal mind is, in fact, something worse than the mind that is malicious or hateful. In a well-expressed and representative statement, Norrie puts the point this way:

"Even if you hate someone that is at least a humanly recognizable emotion. It indicates a moral connection, albeit a bad one, with the hated person. That person is at least worthy of hatred, and there is a kind of warped, *negative* solidarity within it. The problem of the death camps was that even this was ultimately lacking, and this was at the nub of the idea of the banality of evil. Adolf Eichmann's motives were so mundane as to be no real motives at all when compared with the enormity of what he was doing. They revealed in their banality a complete failure to recognize any sense of the human in his victims, to be able to think of his victims as being human."[22]

As we have seen, albeit in different ways, many of the cases of evil undertaken in a moral fog also share the failure to recognize, much less relate accordingly to, others as human, moral beings. Thus, one might similarly (for this reason), regard such minds as evil. The moral fog of evildoing also presents an explanatory account of the failure to recognize one's victims as human – while plodding along and being guided by extraordinarily mundane motives in the circumstances. Moreover, the explanation it gives also helps provide a rationale to justify being able to attribute evil agency to a "fogged up" mind.

partly written – by Orson Welles) in the film noir classic *The Third Man* presents this challenge. In one notable scene with Holly Martins (a friend from the past, again, played by Joseph Cotten), Holly asks Harry (while they are riding a Ferris Wheel!) if Harry has ever seen any of the victims of his black-market profiteering in adulterated deadly medicines. Harry opens the door of the carriage, telling Holly to look down, and replies: "Would you feel any pity if one of those dots stopped moving forever? If I offered you 20,000 pounds for every dot that stopped – would you, really, old man, tell me to keep my money? Or would you calculate how many dots you could afford to spare? Free of income tax, old man...," *The Third Man*, Rialto Pictures, 1949.

[22] Norrie, *op. cit.*, p. 90.

Consider how the phenomena of screening off, or inverting moral claims, that we describe as moral fog, not only defeats these claims, but does so by rendering them irrelevant, or seemingly false, without anything like reflective judgment or dialogue. In this way, since it pulls the rug from underneath these building blocks of the prosocial, moral life, the moral fog is a fundamental threat to the prosocial, moral enterprise. As such, we ought to be able to attribute evil to a "fogged up" mind, due to its disabling of basic capacities required for prosocial and moral regard for one another.[23]

We can be pluralists about evil minds or character, just as most philosophers nowadays are about good minds or character. While those we imagine to be aiming at evil, or to be moved by antisocial extremes, such as malice or hate, or who, at least understand that their conduct is evil, have a long-standing place in the annals of evil minds, so do, or so ought to, many cases of those who are in a moral fog such that they really don't recognize, and so don't really care about, the evil they do.

5.5 Nothing New Under the Sun

Is evil online really anything new? Although the Internet provides a significant forum for evil, some seem to think that it is not in any important, distinctive way creating or expressing anything new. In Chapter 3, we canvassed, and rejected, this claim, as it had been made in relation to online sex predation of young people. However, one might think that generally, allowing for some exceptions, there is not much new under the sun, so far as disturbing, crazy or evil conduct goes.

[23] This will, of course, be a matter of degree depending upon the particular case. We are also not suggesting that an episode or period of evildoing, including from what might be described as a "fogged up," but nevertheless, evil mind, thereby makes for an evil person or character. As we have seen, there are many cases, both online and from our traditional worlds, where people of generally relatively prosocial, moral character have lost their way, say, for a time, in certain circumstances.

The first and most obvious problem with thinking this way, is that there are just too many exceptions. We only need consider the explosion in new ways to go mad, as Carl Elliott put it (way back in 2000), regarding perversions created and sustained online. As described in Chapter 2, Elliott researched the online phenomenon of "apotemnophilia" – where people associate, and reinforce to one another in online communities, positive images, usually sexual images, with amputating their limbs – and we saw a number of such cases (new ways to go mad) in Chapter 1.

Second, however, and perhaps more damning (than even a very long list of fairly esoteric new perversions, and so on), has been the explosion in, and changing forms of, some of our far more common, and long-standing problems. Online bullying, for instance, especially amongst adolescents, is by now one of the most widely researched and studied examples, and has obviously exploded, and brought notable new forms of bullying.[24] Online bullies now have greater access to their victims via the virtual world, employing an array of technological means to do so. The Internet, mobile and texting, file and photo-sharing, email and chat sites are all often, and at once, involved. Online bullying moves well past the school yard, to infiltrate the privacy and safety of the teenager's home or bedroom. The bullying is often relentless and siege-like, with the victim being attacked all hours of the day or night. The collusion of others in the bullying is quickly enlisted online, and, as we have seen, this is all dangerously empowered by a medium where, for example, there is seeming isolation and little or nil social transaction costs for how one behaves. A medium where many of the negative reactions and sanctions of others that would otherwise apply in response to such conduct, get little or no voice.

Moreover, as a result, an important aspect of what is "new under the sun" here, is not only that *how* one can be bullied has changed, and that the occurrence and impact of bullying has exploded, but that the typical drivers of online bullying have changed. As we

---

[24] Recall, similarly, our discussion of online shaming in Chapter 1.

have seen across various types of cases, online bullies – unlike what is typically true in our traditional worlds – are often barely, if at all, aware that their online attacks have significant immediate and cumulative impacts.

For a quite different, but equally striking, example of how new drivers for common, age-old, crimes have appeared online, consider the moral fog of apparent "unreality" of online use that characterizes Nick Leeson's account of his conduct, when as an employee, he was the root cause of the collapse of Barings Bank. Looking back on his gigantic computer-assisted fraud, Leeson admitted that his illegal and almost daily transfers of enormous sums of money was enabled by the air of unreality his "virtual" world transactions had about them. They seemed just another set of characters on his computer screen and data streams accommodated by data bases. As a result, they did not trigger moral feelings, or reminiscences of duties and moral commitments, *at all.*[25] Again, the relevance and guiding role of moral understanding in the circumstances was, in part, screened from view by the medium.

5.6 The Liberal

Many recognize that the Internet is an anarchic and unregulated and uncontrollable environment, but argue that this is exactly why it is so valuable. "Information wants to be free" is the adage of some of its early adaptors and staunch defenders of freedom of expression and information. The objection here is usually developed by appeal to liberal views concerning individual rights and freedoms, enabling and respecting the choices of people (enabling them to be, and respecting them as, consenting adults), and the flourishing of a deliberative democracy, i.e., where people have a range of information and lifestyles upon which to deliberate and choose.

Of course, notions of "consenting adults," "lifestyle choices" or a "deliberative democracy" hardly apply in many cases of evil online, such as online bullying or terrorist murders. There are various

[25] Nick Leeson, *Rogue Trader: The Original Story of the Banker who Broke the System*, London: Sphere, 1996.

disturbing cases, however, where such notions have been, or might be, claimed to apply. Such as, for example, cases of engaging in sexual cannibalism online, collective Internet suicide pacts, glorifications of anorexia, or the uploading of images of victims of violence and accidents for entertainment purposes. While such cases are seemingly (plainly) fairly disturbed or bad, one might nevertheless think they should be permitted, and that forums for their expression should continue to be available. (Again, along something like the lines of the need to provide a mixed and broad landscape of human attitudes and conduct, in order to enable and respect people's capacities for informed understanding and reflection, and, in turn, provide the foundation stones needed for a flourishing deliberative democracy.[26]) On the other hand, environments that permit, much less stimulate and support, such extremes of self-destructive behaviors and antisocial attitudes and conduct, tend, unsurprisingly, to quickly collapse into significantly dysfunctional worlds – rather than help us achieve anything like a flourishing deliberative democracy.

But perhaps this is fairly obvious and uncontroversial, and most of us would not seek to defend the availability of such material online, or anywhere else. There are, however, many "grey" areas, such as the ready availability of adult pornography. It is far more common in such cases, where there is much less widespread agreement about whether the activity is even bad, much less evil, to find people concerned about freedom of speech, pursuits and lifestyles. And so it is common in discussions about the lack of regulation online to hear commentators express their concern about how filters and other measures aimed to prohibit the availability of such material would be a serious violation of our rights and so on.

This liberal view has most plausibility if you imagine responsible, well-adjusted adults with no significant experience of limitations,

[26] John Stuart Mill's "experiments in living" provide one very well-known expression of such a view in relation to how we learn the good. See J. S. Mill, *On Liberty*, Vol. 18, *The Collected Works of J. S. Mill*, ed. J. M. Robson, Toronto, University of Toronto Press, 1977, pp. 260–267. For concrete suggestions of how to enhance diversity and plurality and prevent filter bubbles, see Bozdag, E. & van den Hoven, 'Breaking the Filter Bubble: Democracy and Design, J. Ethics Inf Technol (2015) 17: 249. https://doi.org/10.1007/s10676-015-9380-y.

weakness, vice and problem circumstances. Few of us, however, have lived free of such things, and free of their negative impact upon our attitudes and conduct. Many of the cases of an apparent fall in to self-destructive, corrupting or evil conduct online, have involved people who were experiencing a period of, say, depression, or isolation, within the overall context of an otherwise relatively normal life. Nevertheless, you might still think this should not win the day against the ability of you (and other more well-adjusted members of the community) to access and choose all sorts of material and pursuits easily.

But, of course, it is not just about you. You might think firearms should be available to responsible adults. You might think that pornography, alcohol and perhaps many other drugs should be available. You might think you should have easy access to all of them, and more, in the domestic comfort of your own home. And you might justify your thoughts by appeal to liberal considerations to do with your rights as an individual to have choice, and to be able to (fairly easily) act on it – otherwise, to the extent you cannot do what you choose, you don't really have much choice do you? But even if this argument for easy access made sense in a "world of your own" (or with only other very well-adjusted adults), there are other fairly obvious, often conflicting and more compelling, considerations, that win the day when the world you inhabit is not your own.[27]

So, for instance, while you, in a world of your own, might have a legitimate claim to quite unrestricted access to your whisky, porn, or guns, this does not mean that you would leave your whisky, porn, much less gun, sitting on the coffee table in your house when you know there are children or young people around. You put your whisky, porn, or gun out of harm's way. If you don't and, for instance, your child makes themselves sick drinking your whisky left on the coffee table, you are not going to defend your carelessness by appeal

[27] Of course, from a concern for personal safety, many argue that it is precisely because we are not in a world of our own, but instead are in one where many people have guns, and they are not all "well-adjusted," that we also need, or have a right to, firearms ourselves.

to your right to have a drink. Similarly, if you knew that people with significant mental health issues were in the house, you would not think it acceptable that you leave some guns and ammunition lying around, even if you think, and even if you were right to think, that *you*, considered in isolation, should be able to have guns lying around the house. Of course, in many online social worlds, all sorts of people can be "in the house."

Since then, we do not imagine that an appeal to liberal values in our traditional worlds trumps the concerns that we have, as reflected in our laws, rules, social conventions and settled moral judgments, about widespread, undiscriminating, easy availability and access to, say, pornography, guns, or alcohol, it is hard to see why we should imagine that an appeal to liberal values should win the day in virtual worlds provided online.

5.7 Conclusion: Just Me and the Internet

Under questioning at his trial, Dylann Storm Roof, the mass murderer described in Chapter 1, confessed to being a white supremacist, and claimed:

> I had to do it, because somebody had to do something… Black people are killing white people every day on the streets, and they rape white women, a hundred white women a day. The fact of the matter is what I did was so minuscule to what they're doing to white people… (When asked what made him think this way, he said)… The first thing that woke me up was the Trayvon Martin case. I kept hearing about this kid, and for some reason after I read an article I typed the words "black on white crime" into a search. And that was it. (and when asked "was it just you, or was there someone else?" he replied)… Just me, and the Internet.[28]

---

[28] Edward Ball reporting on the trial against Roof, *New York Review of Books*, LXIV, no 5, 23 March 2017, pp. 12–16.

In recent years, the need to design our worlds with our values in mind first, rather than wonder what has happened to them later, has become increasingly recognized.[29] While the moral life is under threat from those who are antisocial and immoral in character, bad conduct commonly also issues from people not already so inclined. Thus, our efforts to better design our worlds, notably through law, regulation, education and social conventions, face a far bigger, more complex problem than identifying and addressing those already disposed from extremes of ill-will or self-conceit. Many of us, otherwise relatively prosocial and moral people, may, depending upon the character of our relationships with others and the impact of our settings, also run amok and undermine the moral life.

Many social scientists and philosophers looking at this area have been led to either deny moral character exists (or claim it is largely irrelevant to whether one acts rightly or wrongly), or to highlight the need for good moral character, where this is understood as a force to question, and where needed, stand up against, the influence of the external world.[30] We have not denied that the latter view of good moral character has a fundamental place. There are many aspects to, indeed pictures of, good moral character, including ones that seem to conflict in certain ways. We have argued, however, that our capacities for moral imagination and understanding are more in the hands of others and features of our settings than most of us normally think.

[29] See, for example, Batya Friedman, Peter H. Khan Jnr., Alan Borning, Alina Huldtgren, Value-sensitive design and information systems, *Early Engagement and New Technologies: Opening up the Laboratory*, 16, December, 2013, pp. 55–95. Batya Friedman is the pioneer of the recent value-sensitive-design approach. For some very recent work see: Value Sensitive Design: Theory, Method and Practise, Batya Friedman and David Hendry (eds), Cambridge, MA., MIT Press, 2018, and; Designing in Ethics, Jeroen van den Hoven, Seumas Miller and Thomas Pogge (eds), Cambridge, U.K., Cambridge University Press, 2017.

[30] This, of course, is not to say these approaches are incompatible. We might, for instance, think that while moral character, so understood, does not exist, that this is nevertheless how moral character should be understood. And obviously, and perhaps more commonly, we may simply think it that rare and that we need more of it.

In particular, in looking at the flourishing of evil online, we have highlighted the negative impact of features of our communication settings, and how this shapes self-expression and interaction with one another. An impact we have described as creating forms of moral fog that block out, screen off and sometimes overturn appropriate moral understanding.

Our online-transformed worlds have delivered new and widespread forms of moral fog that limit and negatively shape moral imagination and understanding. To this extent, they often present new and widespread forms of hermeneutic injustice[31] for individuals and communities. Those who are antecedently of ill-will, mentally unstable, or morally immature, are obviously prone to have the problems of their situation compounded. But none of us are perfect, and many varieties of moral fog, such as enabled by the rise of fake news, or the demolition of public/private worlds online, plainly impact upon us all.

One aspect of evil online, such as very obviously illustrated by the problem of fake news, raises important concerns about the fate of knowledge acquisition for individuals, and so of individual understanding and self-governance, and the fate of democracy that is built upon all of this.[32] This presents one notable problem of hermeneutic injustice concerning how we can understand and give meaning to our lives, and so one notable threat to the moral life. Indeed, the problem is not just that the rational capacities of individuals are becoming increasingly fogged up by the deluge of lies, made up stories and ridiculous things that pass as news stories, such as the mundane

[31] Miranda Fricker coined the term to describe how collective social understanding can be structured (by those in power) to obscure the experiences of people from the collective social understanding, and so undermine their capacity to make sense of their experiences. See her book, Epistemic Injustice, Power and the Ethics of Knowing, Oxford, U.K., Oxford University Press, 2007.

[32] Many are now having such concerns. See, for example, Dirk Helbing, et al., Will democracy survive big data and artificial intelligence? *Scientific American*, February 2017, https://www.scientificamerican.com/article/will-democracy-survive-big-data-and-artificial-intelligence/ (accessed 22 November 2017).

details of the personal lives of celebrities. The problem, as many are recognizing, is also that, as a result, there seems a widespread cultural malaise of disinterest about what's true, and so about reality, and about reflecting and developing as a person, and so about taking one another (including oneself) seriously as persons.

We have also seen a range of other, quite different, problems for moral understanding, and problems for the meaning we can give our lives.[33] Thus, in addition to worries about exercising our reasoning capacities in worlds where the delivery of information makes it very difficult to tell fact from fiction, we have seen how online worlds can collapse and deform a range of basic prosocial values, including important aspects of intimacy, trust, autonomy and privacy. Accordingly, to the extent that our capacities to give meaning to our lives by being able to create and sustain such values slides from view, our online-transformed worlds deliver significant forms of hermeneutic injustice to individuals and communities in these ways also.

The problem of "Just me and the Internet" does not apply only to Dylann Storm Roof, and others whose lives are already deeply troubled. As we saw in Chapter 2, the architecture of online worlds – including the filter bubbles, recommender systems, user profiles and search algorithms – all work to enable users to seemingly create and live in a world (much more) on their own terms. This is how these mechanisms shape our pursuit of interests, our activities, and our self-expression and communication. At the same time, however, other aspects of this online architecture, along with various features of our online life-worlds (as we also saw in Chapter 2), are also shaping how we pursue our lives and how we seemingly do so "on our own terms."

If we want to better design our worlds with our values in mind first, rather than wonder what has happened to them later, then we need to first take some stock of, and get clearer about, the nature of

---

[33] For recent efforts on some design solutions and future directions to help deal with cases of emotional trauma and problems due to online conduct, such as from bullying, see, for example, discussion of the empathy app, http://www.theverge.com/2017/3/2/14764620/koko-social-network-mental-health-depression-app-kik (accessed 22 November 2017).

our values, and how they are realized. Investigating evil online has led us down both these tracks, and has led us to think of many cases of evildoing as undertaken in a moral fog. The problem is not that we cannot "tell Heaven from Hell." However problems for normative competence brought by moral fog are many and varied and present far more of a problem for the moral life than we commonly think. So, for example, with the pursuit of intimacy, and our reliance upon elders and experts, problems of moral fog are (often) unavoidable. However it is upon such attachments and forms of reliance upon one another that we create and sustain much of the prosocial, moral life. Similarly, some varieties of moral fog are an unavoidable risk of living in our traditional plural worlds of face-to-face shared activity and communication. Worlds that enable some of the important aspects of our basic values, such as intimacy, privacy and autonomy, but where, for example, the likes of *Dangerous Liaisons* may also thrive.

However, by changing and demolishing so much of this landscape, our online-transformed worlds have magnified problems of moral fog and created many new ones. Problems, unlike in our traditional worlds and without the history of settled moral judgments, conventions and so forth, that we have developed over the ages to help us navigate our way, and so to help us to tell Heaven from Hell. There is not really any going back, in the sense of going back to some pre-Internet world. So if we want to address problems to do with the demise of our moral values and the obfuscation of moral fog, we will need to find ways to do so in our online-transformed worlds. As just noted, some such value-sensitive design work is currently being done. Hopefully our discussion, in particular of how even our "better angels" may descend into evil, provides some groundwork to guide future value-sensitive approaches to the use and design of our online-transformed worlds.

Bibliography

Excluding film and television references and links to online reports.

Adams, Robert, M. *A Theory of Virtue: Excellence in Being for the Good*. Oxford: Clarendon Press, 2006.

Aitken, Mary. *The Cyber Effect: A Pioneering Cyberpsychologist Explains How Human Behaviour Changes Online*. London: John Murray, 2016.

Alfano, Mark. *Character as Moral Fiction*. Cambridge: Cambridge University Press, 2013.

Arendt, Hannah. *Eichmann in Jerusalem: A Report on the Banality of Evil*. London: Penguin, 1964.

Arendt, Hannah. *Hannah Arendt: The Last Interview and Other Conversations*. New York: Melville House Publishing, 2013.

Arendt, Hannah. *Origins of Totalitarianism*. New York: Harcourt Brace 1968.

Aristotle. *The Nicomachean Ethics*, trans. W. D. Ross. Oxford: Oxford University Press, 1980.

Aristotle. *Magna Moralia*, trans. W. D. Ross. Oxford: Clarendon Press, 1915.

Asch, S. E. Effects of group pressure upon the modification and distortion of judgment, in H. Guetzkow (ed.), *Groups, Leadership and Men*. Pittsburgh, PA: Carnegie Press, 1951.

Aschheim, Steven. Review of Stangneth, *Eichmann Before Jerusalem*. *New York Times*, Sunday Book Review, 4 December 2014.

Athanassoulis, Nafsika. Virtue ethics. The Internet Encyclopedia of Philosophy, www.iep.utm.edu/virtue.

Ball, Edward. On Dylann Roof. *New York Review of Books*, 9 March 2017 issue.

Baron-Cohen, Simon. *The Science of Evil: On Empathy and the Origins of Cruelty*. New York: Basic Books, 2011.

Evil Online, First Edition. Dean Cocking and Jeroen van den Hoven.

Bartlett, Jamie. *The Dark Net: Inside the Digital Underworld*. London: William Heinemann, 2014.

Baym, Nancy, K. *Personal Connections in a Digital Age*. Cambridge: Polity Press, 2010.

Beatty, Joseph. Thinking and moral considerations: Socrates and Arendt's Eichmann. *The Journal of Value Inquiry*, 10, no. 1, Winter 1976.

Bergen, Peter. *Homegrown United States of Jihad: Investigating America's Homegrown Terrorists*. New York: Crown Publishers, 2016.

Bijker, Wiebe, E., Hughes, Thomas P., and Trevor Pinch (eds), The Social Construction of Technological Systems: New Directions in the Sociology and History of Technology, Cambridge, Mass. MIT Press, 2012.

Boyd, Danah. *Its Complicated: The Social Lives of Networked Teens*. New Haven, CT: Yale University Press, 2014.

Briggle, Adam. Real friends: how the internet can foster friendship. *Ethics and Information Technology*, 10, no. 1, 2008.

Butler, Judith. Hannah Arendt's challenge to Adolf Eichmann. *The Guardian*, August 29 2011, available at https://www.theguardian.com/commentisfree/2011/aug/29/hannah-arendt-adolf-eichmann-banality-of-evil (accessed 18 November 2017).

Calder, Todd. The apparent banality of evil: the relationship between evil acts and evil character. *Journal of Social Philosophy*, 34, no. 3, Fall 2003.

Calder, Todd. Is evil just very wrong? *Philosophical Studies*, 163, 177–196, 2013.

Campbell, John. Can philosophical accounts of altruism accommodate experimental data on helping behavior? *Australasian Journal of Philosophy*, 77, 1999.

Card, Claudia. Kant's theory of radical evil, in Card, 2002. Available at Oxford Scholarship Online, http://www.oxfordscholarship.com/view/10.1093/0195145089.001.0001/acprof-9780195145083-chapter-4

Card, Claudia. *The Atrocity Paradigm: A Theory of Evil*. New York: Oxford University Press, 2002.

Cesarani, David. *Becoming Eichmann: Rethinking the Life, Crimes and Trial of a "Desk Murderer."* Cambridge, MA: Da Capo Press, 2006.

Cesarani, David. *Eichmann: His Life and Crimes*. London: Vintage, 2004.

Cocking, Dean. Aristotle, friendship and virtue. *Revue Internationale de Philosophie*, Societe Belge de Philosophie, 1, pp. 83–90, 2014.

Cocking, Dean. Friendship, in *International Encyclopaedia of Ethics*. Oxford: Wiley-Blackwell, 2013.

Crawford, Christina. *Mommie Dearest*. New York: William Morrow and Co., 1978.

Darley, John, M., and Batson, Daniel, C. "From Jerusalem to Jericho": A study of situational and dispositional variables in helping behavior. *Journal of Personality and Social Psychology*, 27, no. 1, July 1973.

De Laclos, Choderlos. *Dangerous Liaisons*. Harmondsworth: Penguin Classics, 2007. (First published by Durand Neveu, France, 1782.)

Dewey, Caitlin. What "parody," "prank" and other common defenses for dumb internet stunts mean in reality. *Washington Post*, 24 September 2014.

Doris, John. *Lack of Character: Personality and Moral Behavior*. Cambridge: Cambridge University Press, 2002.

Dunphy, Rachel. The abusive "pranks" of YouTube family vloggers. *New York* (Magazine), 28 April 2017.

Ekman, P., and Friesen, W.V. *Unmasking the Face: A Guide to Recognizing Emotions from Facial Cues*. Upper Saddle River, NJ: Prentice Hall, 1975.

Ekman, P., and Rosenberg, E.L. *What the Face Reveals: Basic and Applied Studies of Spontaneous Expression Using the Facial Action Coding System (FACS)*. New York: Oxford University Press, 1997.

Elliott, Carl. A new way to be mad. *The Atlantic Monthly*, December 2000.

Elstein, David. Xunzi. Internet Encyclopedia of Philosophy, www.iep.utm.edu/xunzi

Feinberg, Joel. *The Moral Limits of the Criminal Law*, Vol. 1, *Harm to Others*. Oxford: Oxford University Press. 1984.

Formosa, Paul. Kant on the radical evil of human nature. *The Philosophical Forum*, 38, no. 3, 2007.

Formosa, Paul. Moral responsibility for banal evil. *Journal of Social Philosophy*, 37, no. 4, Winter, 2006.

Frank, R.H. The Darwin Economy: Liberty, Competition and the Common Good. Princeton University Press, U.S., 2011.

Frank, R.H. *What Price the Moral High Ground? Ethical Dilemmas in Competitive Environments*. Princeton, NJ: Princeton University Press, 2004.

Fricker, M. Epistemic Injustice, Power and the Ethics of Knowing. Oxford University Press, 2007.

Friedman, B. and Hendry, D. (eds) Value Sensitive Design: Theory, Method and Practise. MIT Press, 2018.

Friedman, Batya, Khan Jnr, Peter, H., Borning, Alan, Huldtgren, Alina. Value-sensitive design and information systems, in *Early Engagement and New Technologies: Opening up the Laboratory*, vol. 16, (series, Philosophy of Engineering and Technology). Amsterdam: Springer, 2013.

Gardner, Howard, and Davis, Katie. *The App generation. How Today's youth navigate identity, intimacy, and imagination in a digital world*. New Haven, CT: Yale University Press, 2013.

Glover, Jonathan. *Humanity: A Moral History of the Twentieth Century*, 2nd Edition. New Haven, CT: Yale University Press, 2012.

Goffman, Ervin. *The Presentation of Self in Everyday Life*. New York: Doubleday Anchor, 1959.

Goldman, Alvin, I. *Epistemology and Cognition*. Cambridge, MA: Harvard University Press, 1986.

Grenberg, Jeanine. *The Ethics of Humility – A Story of Dependence, Corruption, and Virtue*. Cambridge: Cambridge University Press, 2005.

Guest, Tim. *Second Lives: A Journey Through Virtual Worlds*. New York: Random House, 2008.

Hanson, Erik, M. Immanuel Kant: radical evil. Internet Encyclopedia of Philosophy, www.iep.utm.edu/rad-evil

Harman, Gilbert. Moral philosophy meets social psychology: virtue ethics and the fundamental attribution error. *Proceedings of the Aristotelian Society*, New Series, 99, 1999.

Haslip, Susan. Aristotle's theory of the Good Life: a consideration of the role of luck in the good life and the concept of self-sufficiency. *Quadlibet Journal*, 5, no. 1, January 2003.

Hatzfeld, Jean. *Machete Season: The Killers in Rwanda Speak*. New York: Farrar, Straus, Giroux, 2005; London: Picador, 2006.

Hawthorne, Nathaniel. *The Scarlet Letter*. London: Vintage Books, p. 25. 2008. (Originally published Boston: Ticknor and Fields, (1850).)

Helbing, Dirk, Frey, Bruno, S., Gigerenzer, Gerd, Hafen, Ernst, Hagner, Michael, Hofstetter, Yvonne, van den Hoven, Jeroen, Zicari, Roberto, V., and Zwitter, Andrej. Will democracy survive big data and artificial intelligence? *Scientific American*, February 2017.

Helm, Sarah. *If this is a woman: inside Ravensbruck: Hitler's concentration camp for women*. London: Little, Brown, 2014.

Hilberg, Raul. *The Destruction of the European Jews*. 1st ed. Chicago: Quadrangle Books, 1961.

James, C. Disconnected: Youth, New Media, and the Ethics Gap, Cambridge, MA., MIT Press, 2014.

Johnson, David, R., and Post, David. Law and borders: the rise of law in cyberspace. *First Monday*, 1, no. 1, 1996.

Kaliarnta, Sofia. Using Aristotle's theory of friendship to classify online friendships: a critical counterview. *Ethics and Information Technology*, 18, no. 2, June, 2016.

Kant, Immanuel. What is enlightenment? *The Berlin Monthly*, 1784.

Kant, Immanuel. Religion within the boundaries of mere reason, in Wood, Allen, W., and Di Giovanni, George (trans. and eds.), *Religion and Rational Theology*. Cambridge: Cambridge University Press, 1996.

Kekes, John. *Facing Evil*. Princeton, NJ: Princeton University Press, 1990.

Kernohan, Andrew. Rights against polluters. *Environmental Ethics*, 17, no. 3, Fall 1995.

Kirkpatrick, David. *The Facebook Effect: The Inside Story of the Company that is Connecting the World*. New York: Simon & Schuster, 2010.

Leeson, Nick. *Rogue Trader: The Original Story of the Banker Who Broke the System*. London: Sphere, 1996.

Marsden, John. I was sacked by a serial killer. *Sydney Morning Herald*, 4 September 2004.

Maslow, A. H. A theory of human motivation. *Psychological Review*, 50, no. 4, 1943.

Maslow, A. H. *Motivation and Personality*. New York: Harper, 1954.

Massing, Michael. Trial and error. *New York Times*, Sunday Book Review, 17 October 2004.

McPherson, Miller, Smith-Lovin, Lynn, and Cook, James, M. Birds of a feather: homophily in social networks. *Annual Review of Sociology*, 415–444, 2001.

Milgram, Stanley. The Small World Problem. *Psychology Today*, May 1967.

Mill, J. S., *On Liberty*, Vol. 18, *The Collected Works of J. S. Mill*, ed., J. M. Robson. Toronto: University of Toronto Press, 1977.

Moran, Kate. Delusions of virtue: Kant on self-conceit. *Kantian Review*, 19, no. 03, November 2014.

Morton, Adam. *On Evil: Thinking in Action*. New York: Routledge, 2004.

Murdoch, Iris. *The Black Prince*. Harmondsworth: Penguin, 1973.

Nagel, Thomas. Concealment and exposure. *Philosophy and Public Affairs*, 27, no. 1, Winter 1998.

Neiman, Susan. *Evil in Modern Thought: An Alternative History of Philosophy*. Princeton, NJ: Princeton University Press, 2002.

Nissenbaum, Helen. *Privacy in Context: Technology, Policy and the Integrity of Social Life*. Palo Alto, CA: Stanford University Press, 2010.

Norrie, Alan. The scene and the crime: can critical realists talk about good and evil? *Journal of Critical Realism*, 11, no. 1, 2012.

Nussbaum, Martha. Internet misogyny and objectification, in *The Offensive Internet*. Cambridge, MA: Harvard University Press, 2010.

Oakley, Justin, and Cocking, Dean. *Virtue Ethics and Professional Roles*. Cambridge: Cambridge University Press, 2001.

Ovid. *Metamorphoses.* Trans. David Raeburn. Harmondsworth: Penguin Books, 2004.

Pariser, Eli. *The Filter Bubble: What the Internet is Hiding From You.* London: Penguin Press, 2011.

Perry, Gina. *Behind the Shock Machine: The Untold Story of the Notorious Milgram Psychology Experiments.* Brunswick (Victoria): Scribe, 2012, and (Revised Edition) New York, The New Press, 2013.

Plato. *The Republic of Plato.* trans. Benjamin Jowett. Oxford: Clarendon Press, 1908.

Robert, H. Frank. The Darwin Economy: Liberty, Competition and the Common Good, Princeton University Press, U.S., 2011.

Ronson, Jon. *So You've Been Publicly Shamed?* London: Picador (Pan Macmillan), 2015.

Russell, Daniel. Aristotelian virtue theory: after the person-situation debate. *Revue Internationale De Philosophie*, 68, no. 1, 2014.

Russell, Luke. *Evil: A Philosophical Investigation.* Oxford: Oxford University Press, 2014.

Russell, Luke. Is situationism all bad news? *Utilitas*, 21, no. 4, December, 2009.

Sally, David. A general theory of sympathy, mind-reading, and social interaction, with an application to the Prisoner's Dilemma. *Social Science Information*, 39, no.4, 2000.

Sherman, Nancy. *Making a Necessity of Virtue: Aristotle and Kant on Virtue*, Cambridge: Cambridge University Press, 1997.

Smith, Michael. Beyond belief, desire and rationality, or: the unsettling truth about conditions of responsibility, in Vincent, Nicole, van de Poel, Ibo, and van den Hoven, Jeroen, eds., *Compatibilist Responsibility: Beyond Free Will and Determinism.* New York: Springer Publishing, 2011.

Snow, Nancy, E. *Virtue as Social Intelligence: An Empirically Grounded Theory.* New York: Routledge, 2010.

Stangneth, Bettina. *Eichmann Before Jerusalem: The Unexamined Life of a Mass Murderer.* trans. Ruth Martin, New York: Alfred A Knopf, 2014.

Sunstein, Cass. *Republic.com.* Princeton, NJ: Princeton University Press, 2002.

Tempe, Kevin. Tracing and the epistemic condition of responsibility. *The Modern Schoolman*, 88, nos. 1/2, January/April 2011.

Turkle, Sherry. *Alone Together: Why We Expect More From Technology And Less From Each Other.* New York: Basic Books, 2011.

Van den Hoven, J. Miller, S. and Pogge, T. (eds) Designing in Ethics. Cambridge University Press, 2017.

Velasquez, Manuel, Andre, Claire, Shanks, Thomas S.J., and Meyer, Michael. Conscience and authority. J. Markkula Centre for Applied Ethics, Ethics Resources, December 1988.

Vetlesen, Johan Arne. *Evil and Human Agency: Understanding Collective Evildoing*. Cambridge: Cambridge University Press, 2006.

Voigtlander, Nico, and Voth, Hans-Joachim. Taught to hate: Nazi indoctrination and anti-Semitic beliefs in Germany. *Proceedings of the National Academy of Sciences USA*, 112, no. 26, 2015.

Watson, Gary. Responsibility and the limits of evil: variations on a Strawsonian theme, in Gary Watson, *Agency and Answerability: Selected Essays*. Oxford: Oxford University Press, 2004.

Weimann, Gabriel. *Terror on the Internet: The New Arena, The New Challenges*. Washington, DC: United States Institute for Peace Press, 2006.

Weiss, Geoff. *Tubefilter*, The good, the bad and the fake: the rise of YouTube's Prank video genre. 13 April 2016.

Weizenbaum, Joseph. *Computer Power and Human Reason: From Judgment to Calculation*. San Francisco, W. H. Freeman and Company, 1976.

Wenzl, Roy, Potter, Tim, Kelly, L., and Laviana, Hurst. *Bind, Torture, Kill: The Inside Story of BTK the Guy Next Door*. New York: HarperCollins, 2007.

Wiebe, E. Bijker; Thomas P. Hughes; Trevor Pinch, eds. (1987). "The Social Constructions of Technological Systems. Cambridge, Massachusetts: MIT Press see also https://en.wikipedia.org/wiki/Social_construction_of_technology.

Wishman, Seymour. *Confessions of a Criminal Lawyer: A Memoir*. New York: NY Times Books, 1981.

Wolak, Janis, Finkelhor, David, Mitchell, Kimberly, J., and Ybarra, Michele, L. Online "predators" and their victims: myths, realities, and implications for prevention and treatment. *American Psychologist*, February–March 2008. http://www.unh.edu/ccrc/internet-crimes/Am%20Psy%20Paper%20Highlights.pdf (accessed 10 November 2017).

Wolf, Susan. Sanity and the metaphysics of responsibility, in Ferdinand Schoeman, ed., *Responsibility, Character and the Emotions: New Essays in Moral Psychology*. Cambridge: Cambridge University Press, 1987.

Zimbardo, Philip, G. Power turns good soldiers into bad apples. *Boston Globe,* 9 May 2004.

Zimbardo, Philip, G. *The Lucifer Effect: Understanding How Good People Turn Evil*. New York: Random House, 2007. http://web.archive.org/web/20160322060012/http://www.lucifereffect.com/index.html

Index

Evil Online, First Edition. Dean Cocking and Jeroen van den Hoven.